ANDROID PROGRAMMING FOR BEGINNERS

BEGINNERS

Guides To Build Your First Mobile App

BY CARLOS SMITH

Table of contents

Introduction

Part 1: Setting Up Your Android Development Environment

Part 2: Building User Interfaces with Jetpack Compose

- ## Chapter 4: Introduction to Jetpack Compose
  - 4.1 Compose Fundamentals: Composables and Modifiers
  - 4.2 Building Basic UI Elements (Text, Buttons, Images)
  - 4.3 Previewing Your UI in Android Studio
- ## Chapter 5: Layouts and UI Design
  - 5.1 Working with Layout Composables (Column, Row, Box)
  - 5.2 Creating Responsive and Adaptive UIs
  - 5.3 Applying Material Design 3 Principles
- ## Chapter 6: Handling User Interactions
  - 6.1 Responding to User Events (Button Clicks, Gestures)
  - 6.2 Collecting User Input (TextFields)
  - 6.3 Managing UI State

Part 3: Adding Functionality and Data Management

- ## Chapter 7: Navigation Between Screens
  - 7.1 Implementing Navigation with Navigation Compose
  - 7.2 Passing Data Between Screens
- ## Chapter 8: Data Persistence
  - 8.1 Storing Simple Data with Shared Preferences
  - 8.2 Introduction to ViewModel and StateFlow

Introduction: Your Journey to Becoming an Android Developer

Future Android developer! Welcome to this book, your starting point on an exciting journey into the world of mobile app development. If you've ever looked at your smartphone and wondered, "How did they make that app?" or if you've dreamt of creating your own app that solves a problem or entertains millions, you're in the right place.

I remember when I first started learning Android development. It felt like trying to decipher a secret code. There were so many new terms, tools, and concepts. But, like any skill, it gets easier with practice and the right guidance. That's why I wrote this book – to be the guide I wish I had when I was starting out.

Why Android?

You might be wondering, "Why should I learn Android development?" Well, let's break it down:

- **Massive Reach:** Android powers a vast majority of smartphones worldwide. That means your apps have the potential to reach an enormous audience.
- **High Demand:** Android developers are in high demand across various industries. Learning Android can open doors to exciting career opportunities.
- **Creative Freedom:** Android provides a flexible platform for you to bring your app ideas to life. Whether it's a productivity tool, a game, or a social networking app, the possibilities are endless.

- **Open Source & Community:** Android is built on an open-source foundation, fostering a vibrant and supportive community. You'll find countless resources, tutorials, and forums to help you along the way.

What You'll Learn in This Book

This book is designed to take you from complete beginner to someone who can confidently build their first Android app. We'll focus on practical, hands-on learning, so you'll be coding and building from the very beginning. Here's a sneak peek of what you'll learn:

- **Setting up your development environment:** We'll guide you through installing Android Studio, the official IDE for Android development.
- **Mastering Kotlin and Jetpack Compose:** Kotlin is the modern programming language for Android, and Jetpack Compose is the future of Android UI development. We'll dive into both, making sure you understand the fundamentals.
- **Building user interfaces:** You'll learn how to create engaging and intuitive user interfaces using Jetpack Compose.
- **Handling user input and data:** We'll cover how to respond to user interactions and store data within your app.
- **Navigating between screens:** You'll learn how to create seamless navigation experiences for your users.
- **Connecting to the internet:** We'll explore how to fetch data from APIs and display it in your app.
- **Debugging and testing:** We'll show you how to identify and fix errors in your code.

- **Publishing your app:** Finally, we'll guide you through the process of publishing your app to the Google Play Store.

My Personal Approach

I believe the best way to learn is by doing. That's why this book is filled with practical examples and step-by-step tutorials. I'll also share my personal insights and experiences, highlighting common pitfalls and offering tips for success.

Don't be afraid to experiment and make mistakes. That's how you learn and grow as a developer. Remember, every expert was once a beginner.

What You'll Need

To get started, you'll need:

- A computer (Windows, macOS, or Linux)
- An internet connection
- A willingness to learn and have fun!

Let's Get Started!

Are you ready to embark on your Android development journey? Let's dive into the next chapter and set up your development environment. By the end of this book, you'll have the skills and knowledge to create your own Android apps and bring your ideas to life. I'm excited to have you along for the ride!

Part 1: Setting Up Your Android Development Environment

Chapter 1: Getting Started with Android

Welcome to the first step of your Android development adventure! In this chapter, we'll lay the foundation by exploring what Android is, why it's a fantastic platform to learn, and the modern tools you'll be using.

1.1 Introduction to Android and Its Ecosystem: More Than Just an OS

Let's talk about Android. You might think of it as just the operating system on your phone, but it's much more than that. It's a vast and dynamic ecosystem that shapes how we interact with technology.

What is Android?

At its core, Android is a mobile operating system based on the Linux kernel.Think of the kernel as the engine that powers the OS. But Android isn't just a bare-bones system; it's a complete software stack that includes:

- **Middleware:** These are the software components that sit between the OS and applications, providing essential services.
- **Key Applications:** Core apps like the phone dialer, web browser, and messaging app are integral to the Android experience.
- **Runtime Environment:** This is where Android apps execute, ensuring they run smoothly and efficiently.

The Open-Source Foundation

One of Android's defining features is its open-source nature, primarily under the Android Open Source Project (AOSP).This means:

- Developers have access to the source code, fostering innovation and customization.
- Device manufacturers can tailor Android to their specific hardware.
- A vibrant community contributes to Android's ongoing development.

Google's Influence and the Google Play Ecosystem

While AOSP provides the foundation, Google plays a pivotal role in shaping the Android ecosystem. They:

- Release new Android versions with enhanced features and security.
- Provide the Google Mobile Services (GMS), which include essential apps and services like the Google Play Store.
- Maintain the Google Play Store, the primary distribution channel for Android apps.

This duality—open-source flexibility and Google's powerful ecosystem—is what makes Android so unique.

The Android Ecosystem: A Web of Devices and Users

The Android ecosystem is incredibly diverse, encompassing:

- **Smartphones and Tablets:** The most common Android devices, ranging from budget-friendly to high-end models.
- **Wearables:** Smartwatches and fitness trackers powered by Wear OS.
- **TVs:** Android TV brings the Android experience to the big screen.
- **Automotive:** Android Auto integrates Android into car infotainment systems.
- **IoT Devices:** Android Things (now Android for IoT) extends Android to embedded devices.

This diversity creates a massive user base, making Android an attractive platform for developers.

When I think about the Android ecosystem, I'm struck by its adaptability. I've seen Android used in everything from simple home automation projects to complex industrial applications. This flexibility is a testament to its powerful design.

Key Trends and Considerations:

- **Fragmentation:** The sheer number of Android devices and versions can lead to fragmentation, making it challenging to ensure app compatibility.However, Google's efforts to streamline updates are mitigating this issue.

- **Security:** As Android's popularity grows, so does the need for robust security. Google continuously improves Android's security features to protect users from threats.
- **Accessibility:** Android provides a range of accessibility features to make apps usable for everyone.[17] Developers should prioritize accessibility in their apps.

Android is more than just an operating system; it's a dynamic and evolving ecosystem that connects billions of users worldwide. By understanding its core components and trends, you'll be well-equipped to navigate the world of Android development.

1.2 Understanding Kotlin and Jetpack Compose: The Modern Android Toolkit

Hey there, let's talk about the dynamic duo that's transforming Android development: Kotlin and Jetpack Compose. These technologies are Google's answer to modern, efficient, and enjoyable Android app creation.

Kotlin: The Modern Language of Android

Kotlin is a statically typed, general-purpose programming language that runs on the Java Virtual Machine (JVM). But what makes it so special for Android?

- **Official Language:** Google officially promotes Kotlin as the preferred language for Android development. This means you get excellent support, up-to-date documentation, and a thriving community.

- **Conciseness and Readability:** Kotlin's syntax is more concise and expressive than Java, reducing boilerplate code and making your code easier to read and maintain.
- **Null Safety:** Kotlin's type system helps prevent null pointer exceptions, a common source of bugs in Java.
- **Interoperability with Java:** You can seamlessly integrate Kotlin with existing Java code, making it easy to transition to Kotlin or use existing Java libraries.
- **Coroutines:** Kotlin coroutines simplify asynchronous programming, making it easier to handle background tasks and network requests.

When I switched from Java to Kotlin, it felt like a breath of fresh air. The reduced boilerplate and null safety features significantly improved my productivity and reduced the number of bugs in my code. It is so much easier to both read and write.

Jetpack Compose: The Future of Android UI

Jetpack Compose is Android's modern toolkit for building native user interfaces. It's a declarative UI framework that simplifies UI development and allows you to build beautiful, responsive interfaces with less code.

- **Declarative UI:** Instead of imperatively manipulating UI elements, you describe *what* your UI should look like, and Compose handles *how* to render it.
- **Kotlin-First:** Compose is built entirely in Kotlin, taking advantage of the language's features.

- **Composable Functions:** UI elements are defined as composable functions, which are reusable and composable.
- **State Management:** Compose provides built-in mechanisms for managing UI state, making it easier to build dynamic and interactive UIs.
- **Live Previews:** Android Studio's live previews allow you to see your UI changes in real-time, speeding up development.

Why Kotlin and Jetpack Compose Together?

These two technologies complement each other perfectly.

- **Modern Development:** They represent the future of Android development, providing a more efficient and enjoyable development experience.
- **Improved Productivity:** Kotlin's conciseness and Compose's declarative UI reduce boilerplate code and make development faster.
- **Better Performance:** Compose's efficient rendering engine and Kotlin's optimized code can lead to better app performance.
- **Enhanced User Experience:** Compose's flexible and expressive UI toolkit allows you to create more engaging and user-friendly interfaces.

Key Considerations:

- **Learning Curve:** While Kotlin and Compose are designed to be easier to use than their predecessors, there's still a learning curve.
- **Community Support:** Both Kotlin and Compose have thriving communities, providing ample resources and support.

- **Migration:** If you have an existing app, migrating to Kotlin and Compose can be a gradual process.

1.3 Why Learn Android Development?: A World of Opportunities

Let's talk about why diving into Android development could be one of the best decisions you make. It's not just about coding; it's about unlocking a world of opportunities.

The Sheer Reach of Android

First off, let's address the elephant in the room: Android's market share. It powers a massive percentage of smartphones globally. This means:

- **Vast Audience:** Your apps have the potential to reach billions of users.
- **Global Impact:** You can create apps that solve problems and improve lives on a global scale.

High Demand for Android Developers

Companies of all sizes are looking for skilled Android developers. This translates to:

- **Job Security:** Android developers are in high demand across various industries.
- **Career Growth:** There are numerous opportunities for advancement and specialization.

- **Competitive Salaries:** Android development skills are highly valued in the job market.[5]

I've seen firsthand how the demand for Android developers has grown. It's a field where your skills are constantly in demand, which provides a sense of security and opens doors to exciting career paths.

Entrepreneurial Opportunities

Android development empowers you to turn your app ideas into reality. You can:

- **Build Your Own Apps:** Create apps that solve problems or entertain users.
- **Start a Business:** Launch your own app-based business or startup.
- **Monetize Your Skills:** Earn income through app sales, in-app purchases, or advertising.

Continuous Learning and Growth

The Android ecosystem is constantly evolving, which means:

- **Stay Up-to-Date:** You'll always be learning new technologies and techniques.
- **Develop Problem-Solving Skills:** You'll face challenges that require creative solutions.
- **Enhance Your Portfolio:** You'll build a portfolio of apps that showcase your skills.

Personal Satisfaction and Creative Expression

There's a unique sense of satisfaction in creating something that people use and enjoy. You can:

- **Bring Your Ideas to Life:** Turn your app ideas into tangible products.
- **Make a Difference:** Create apps that solve real-world problems.
- **Express Your Creativity:** Design and develop apps that reflect your unique style.

For me, the most rewarding aspect of Android development is seeing my apps in the hands of users. Knowing that my work is making a difference is incredibly fulfilling.

Key Considerations:

- **Learning Curve:** Android development can be challenging, but the rewards are well worth the effort.
- **Constant Updates:** The Android ecosystem is constantly evolving, so you'll need to stay up-to-date with the latest technologies.[7]
- **Competition:** The app market is competitive, so you'll need to create high-quality apps that stand out.

Learning Android development is an investment in your future. It provides a wealth of opportunities, from job security and entrepreneurial ventures to personal satisfaction and creative expression. If you're looking for a challenging and rewarding career, Android development is a great choice.

Chapter 2: Installing and Configuring Android Studio

Welcome to the hands-on part of our journey! In this chapter, we'll get your development environment set up by installing Android Studio, exploring its interface, creating your first project, and configuring your emulators and devices.

2.1 Downloading and Installing Android Studio: Your Development Hub

Let's get you set up with Android Studio, the official Integrated Development Environment (IDE) for Android development. Think of it as your coding workshop, where you'll bring your app ideas to life.

Why Android Studio?

Before we dive into the installation process, let's talk about why Android Studio is the go-to tool for Android developers:

- **Official Support:** It's developed and maintained by Google, ensuring you have access to the latest tools and features.
- **Comprehensive Features:** It provides everything you need for Android development, from code editing and debugging to UI design and testing.
- **Integration with Android SDK:** It seamlessly integrates with the Android Software Development Kit (SDK), which contains the libraries and tools necessary for building Android apps.
- **Emulator Support:** It includes a powerful Android emulator for testing your apps on virtual devices.

- **Jetpack Compose Support:** It has excellent support for Jetpack Compose, Android's modern UI toolkit.

Downloading Android Studio

1. **Head to the Official Website:**
   - Open your web browser and go to the official Android Studio download page: developer.android.com/studio.
   - This ensures you're getting the latest and most secure version.
2. **Download the Correct Version:**
   - The website should automatically detect your operating system (Windows, macOS, or Linux).
   - Click the download button to get the appropriate installer.

Installation Process

1. **Run the Installer:**
   - Once the download is complete, run the installer.
   - Follow the on-screen instructions.
2. **Choose Components:**
   - During the installation, you'll be prompted to choose components.
   - Make sure the following are selected:
     - **Android SDK:** This is essential for compiling and running your Android apps.

- **Android Virtual Device (AVD):** This allows you to create and manage Android emulators.
  - You may also want to install the Android SDK Platform-Tools.

3. **Configure SDK Location:**
   - You'll be asked to choose a location for the Android SDK.
   - Select a directory with enough space.
   - Note this location, as you may need it later.

4. **Complete the Installation:**
   - Let the installer do its thing. This may take some time, depending on your internet speed and computer performance.

I remember the first time I installed Android Studio, it felt like a significant step. It's a large piece of software, but it's incredibly powerful. Be patient during the installation process, and make sure you have a stable internet connection.

Post-Installation Tips

- **Update Android Studio:** After installation, check for updates by going to "Help" > "Check for Updates."
- **Configure SDK Manager:** Use the SDK Manager to download additional SDK components and platform versions.
- **Explore the Interface:** Take some time to explore the Android Studio interface and familiarize yourself with its features.

Troubleshooting

- **Insufficient Disk Space:** Ensure you have enough disk space for Android Studio and the Android SDK.
- **Internet Connection Issues:** A stable internet connection is required for downloading components.
- **Firewall or Antivirus Interference:** Temporarily disable your firewall or antivirus software if you encounter issues.

Installing Android Studio is the first step in your Android development journey. By following these steps, you'll have your development environment set up and ready to go. Remember to keep Android Studio and the Android SDK updated to take advantage of the latest features and improvements.

2.2 Exploring the Android Studio Interface: Your Coding Command Center

Now that you've got Android Studio installed, let's take a tour of its interface. Think of it as your coding command center, where you'll spend most of your time building your Android apps.

The Welcome Screen

When you first launch Android Studio, you'll be greeted with the welcome screen. This screen provides quick access to:

- **New Project:** Create a new Android project.

- **Open:** Open an existing project.

- **Get from VCS:** Import a project from a version control system (like Git).

- **Configure:** Customize Android Studio settings.

- **Plugins:** Manage and install plugins.

The Main Window

Once you open a project, you'll see the main Android Studio window, which is organized into several key areas:

- **Toolbar:**
  - Located at the top, it provides quick access to frequently used actions like running, debugging, and building your app.
  - Look for the green "Run" arrow and the bug icon for "Debug."

- **Navigation Bar:**
  - Below the toolbar, it shows the path to the currently open file and provides quick navigation between files.

- **Project Tool Window:**
  - Located on the left, it displays the structure of your project files and folders.
  - You can switch between different views, such as "Android" and "Project."

- **Editor Window:**
  - The central area where you write your code.
  - It provides features like syntax highlighting, code completion, and error checking.

- It also contains the split view for previewing Jetpack Compose.
- **Tool Windows (Bottom and Sides):**
    - These windows provide access to various tools and features, such as:
        - **Logcat:** Displays system messages and app logs, essential for debugging.
        - **Gradle Console:** Shows the progress of Gradle builds.
        - **Terminal:** Provides a command-line interface.
        - **Build:** displays build information.
        - **Layout Inspector:** Shows the layout hierarchy of running apps.
        - **Profiler:** shows performance information.
- **Status Bar:**
    - Located at the bottom, it displays information about the current state of Android Studio.

Key Interface Features

- **Code Completion:**
    - Android Studio provides intelligent code completion, suggesting code snippets and variable names as you type.
    - This can significantly speed up your coding process.
- **Syntax Highlighting:**
    - Different code elements are displayed in different colors, making your code easier to read and understand.
- **Refactoring Tools:**
    - Android Studio provides tools for refactoring your code, such as renaming variables, extracting methods, and moving files.

- This helps you keep your code clean and maintainable.
- **Debugging Tools:**
  - Android Studio's debugger allows you to set breakpoints, inspect variables, and step through your code.
  - This is essential for finding and fixing bugs.

When I first started using Android Studio, I was a bit overwhelmed by all the different windows and features. But as I spent more time with it, I realized how powerful and efficient it is. Take the time to explore the interface and customize it to your liking.

Tips for Customization

- **Keyboard Shortcuts:** Learn and use keyboard shortcuts to speed up your workflow.
- **Themes:** Customize the appearance of Android Studio by changing the theme.
- **Plugins:** Install plugins to add new features and functionality.
- **Window Layout:** Arrange the tool windows to suit your preferences.

2.3 Creating Your First Android Project: Your Initial Steps

Now that you're familiar with the Android Studio interface, let's take the plunge and create your first Android project. This is where your app ideas start to become a reality.

Why Create a New Project?

Creating a new project sets up the basic structure and configuration for your Android app. This includes:

- **Project Files and Folders:** Android Studio generates the necessary files and folders for your app.
- **Gradle Configuration:** Gradle is the build system that automates the process of compiling and packaging your app.
- **Basic Activity Setup:** It creates a basic activity (screen) that you can start building upon.

Steps to Create a New Project

1. **Open Android Studio:**
   - Launch Android Studio.
   - If you're on the welcome screen, click "New Project."
   - If you're already in a project, go to "File" > "New" > "New Project...".

2. **Select a Template:**
   - You'll be presented with a selection of project templates.
   - For beginners, selecting "Empty Compose Activity" is the recommended path. This will give a project that is already setup to use Jetpack Compose.
   - Click "Next."

3. **Configure Your Project:**
   - **Name:** Give your project a meaningful name (e.g., "MyFirstApp").

- **Package Name:** This is a unique identifier for your app (e.g., "com.example.myfirstapp"). It should follow the reverse domain name convention.
- **Save Location:** Choose where you want to save your project.
- **Language:** Ensure "Kotlin" is selected.
- **Minimum SDK:** Choose the minimum Android SDK version that your app will support. This determines the oldest Android version your app can run on. Choosing a lower minimum SDK allows your app to run on more devices, but you may miss out on newer features. Selecting a recent sdk, will allow you to use newer features, but limit the devices that can run your application.
- Click "Finish."

4. **Gradle Sync:**
   - Android Studio will now generate your project and sync it with Gradle.
   - This may take a few moments, depending on your internet speed and computer performance.
   - Be patient during this process.

Understanding the Project Structure

Once your project is created, you'll see the project structure in the "Project" tool window. Key folders include:

- app/src/main/java/: Contains your Kotlin source code.

- app/src/main/res/: Contains your app's resources, such as layouts, images, and strings.
- app/AndroidManifest.xml: The manifest file that defines your app's components and permissions.
- build.gradle **(Project and Module):** Gradle build configuration files.

The first time I created an Android project, I was curious about all the files and folders. Don't worry if it seems overwhelming at first. As you progress, you'll become more familiar with the project structure.

Tips and Considerations:

- **Project Naming:** Choose a descriptive and easy-to-remember project name.
- **Package Name:** Ensure your package name is unique and follows the recommended convention.
- **Minimum SDK:** Consider your target audience when choosing the minimum SDK.
- **Gradle Sync:** If you encounter any issues during Gradle sync, try cleaning and rebuilding your project ("Build" > "Clean Project" and "Build" > "Rebuild Project").

Creating your first Android project is a significant milestone. You've now set up the foundation for building your app. Take some time to explore the project structure and familiarize yourself with the generated files. In the next steps, we'll start building your app's UI and adding functionality.

2.4 Setting Up Emulators and Physical Devices: Testing Your App

Now that you've got your project set up, it's time to test your app. You'll need either an emulator or a physical device for this. Let's explore how to set up both.

Why Testing is Crucial

Testing is essential for ensuring that your app works correctly on different devices and Android versions. It helps you:

- **Identify Bugs:** Find and fix errors in your code.
- **Ensure Compatibility:** Verify that your app works on various screen sizes and Android versions.
- **Test Performance:** Evaluate your app's performance and identify areas for optimization.
- **Get User Feedback:** Test your app with real users to gather feedback and improve its usability.

Setting Up an Android Emulator

An emulator is a virtual device that simulates an Android device on your computer. It's a convenient way to test your app without needing a physical device.

1. **Open the AVD Manager:**
   - In Android Studio, click the AVD (Android Virtual Device) Manager icon in the toolbar (it looks like a phone with an Android logo).

2. **Create a Virtual Device:**

   o Click "Create Virtual Device...".

3. **Select Hardware:**

   o Choose a hardware profile (e.g., Pixel 7, Pixel 6, etc.).

   o Click "Next."

4. **Select System Image:**

   o Choose a system image (Android version) that you want to emulate.

   o If you don't have the system image, click "Download" next to the desired image.

   o Click "Next."

5. **Configure Settings (Optional):**

   o You can customize the virtual device's settings, such as its name, startup size and orientation.

   o Click "Finish."

6. **Run the Emulator:**

   o In the AVD Manager, click the green "Play" button next to your virtual device.

   o The emulator will launch, and you can run your app on it.

Emulators are incredibly useful for quick testing during development. However, they can be resource-intensive, so make sure your computer has enough RAM and processing power.

Setting Up a Physical Device

Testing on a physical device provides a more realistic testing experience.

1. **Enable Developer Options:**
   - On your Android device, go to "Settings" > "About phone."
   - Tap "Build number" seven times.
   - You'll see a message saying "You are now a developer!"

2. **Enable USB Debugging:**
   - Go to "Settings" > "System" (or "Developer options").
   - Enable "USB debugging."

3. **Connect Your Device:**
   - Connect your Android device to your computer using a USB cable.

4. **Allow USB Debugging:**
   - You may be prompted to allow USB debugging on your device.
   - Check the box "Always allow from this computer" and tap "OK."

5. **Run Your App:**
   - In Android Studio, click the "Run" button.
   - Select your physical device from the list of available devices.
   - Your app will run on your physical device.

Testing on physical devices is essential for ensuring that your app works correctly in real-world scenarios. I've found that testing on a variety of devices can uncover issues that are difficult to find using emulators alone.

Tips and Considerations:

- **Emulator Performance:** If your emulator is slow, try increasing the RAM allocation or using hardware acceleration.

- **Physical Device Drivers:** Make sure you have the correct USB drivers installed for your physical device.

- **Device Compatibility:** Test your app on a variety of devices and Android versions to ensure compatibility.

- **Troubleshooting:** If you encounter any issues, check the Android Studio documentation or search for solutions online.

Setting up emulators and physical devices is an essential part of the Android development process. By testing your app thoroughly, you can ensure that it works correctly and provides a great user experience. Remember to test on a variety of devices and Android versions to maximize compatibility.

Chapter 3: Project Structure and Fundamentals

Now that you have Android Studio installed and your first project created, let's take a closer look at the project structure and the fundamental files that make your Android app tick. Understanding these elements is crucial for building robust and maintainable apps.

3.1 Understanding the Android Project Directory: Your App's Blueprint

Having created your first Android project, let's explore its directory structure. Think of it as the blueprint of your app, where all the essential files and folders reside.

Why Understanding the Project Directory Matters

Understanding the project directory is crucial for:

- **Efficient Navigation:** Easily find and manage your app's files.
- **Effective Collaboration:** Work with other developers on the same project.
- **Troubleshooting:** Quickly identify and resolve issues.
- **Customization:** Modify and extend your app's functionality.

Key Folders and Files

1. app/ **Folder:**
   - This folder contains the core components of your app.
2. app/src/main/ **Folder:**

- This folder holds the main source code and resources for your app.

3. app/src/main/java/ **Folder:**
   - This folder contains your Kotlin source code files.
   - The package name you specified during project creation is reflected in the folder structure.
   - Example: com.example.myfirstapp/

4. app/src/main/res/ **Folder:**
   - This folder contains your app's resources, such as layouts, images, and strings.
   - app/src/main/res/drawable/ **Folder:**
     - Stores image files and other drawable resources.
   - app/src/main/res/values/ **Folder:**
     - Stores simple values, such as strings, colors, and themes.
     - strings.xml: Contains string resources.
     - colors.xml: Contains color resources.
     - themes.xml: Contains theme definitions.

5. app/AndroidManifest.xml **File:**
   - This file is the manifest file, which provides essential information about your app to the Android system.
   - It declares components, permissions, and other configurations.

6. build.gradle **(Project Level):**
   - This file defines build configurations that apply to the entire project.

7. app/build.gradle **(Module Level):**
   - This file defines build configurations specific to the app module.
   - It includes dependencies, build types, and other settings.

Practical Implementation: Exploring the strings.xml **File**

Let's explore the strings.xml file, which is located in app/src/main/res/values/. This file stores string resources that you can use in your app.

1. **Open** strings.xml**:**
   - In Android Studio, navigate to app/src/main/res/values/ and open strings.xml.
2. **Add a String Resource:**
   - Add a new string resource to the file.
   - Example:
3. XML

```xml
<resources>

  <string name="app_name">MyFirstApp</string>

  <string name="welcome_message">Welcome to My First App!</string>

</resources>
```

4. **Use the String Resource in Compose:**
   - Open your main activity file (e.g., MainActivity.kt) located in app/src/main/java/com.example.myfirstapp/.
   - Use the string resource in a Text composable.
   - Example:
5. Kotlin

```kotlin
import android.os.Bundle

import androidx.activity.ComponentActivity

import androidx.activity.compose.setContent

import androidx.compose.foundation.layout.fillMaxSize

import androidx.compose.material3.MaterialTheme

import androidx.compose.material3.Surface

import androidx.compose.material3.Text

import androidx.compose.runtime.Composable

import androidx.compose.ui.Modifier

import androidx.compose.ui.res.stringResource

import androidx.compose.ui.tooling.preview.Preview

import com.example.myfirstapp.R

import com.example.myfirstapp.ui.theme.MyFirstAppTheme


class MainActivity : ComponentActivity() {

    override fun onCreate(savedInstanceState: Bundle?) {

        super.onCreate(savedInstanceState)

        setContent {
```

```kotlin
    MyFirstAppTheme {

        Surface(

            modifier = Modifier.fillMaxSize(),

            color = MaterialTheme.colorScheme.background

        ) {

            Greeting(stringResource(id = R.string.welcome_message))

        }

    }

    }

}


@Composable

fun Greeting(name: String, modifier: Modifier = Modifier) {

    Text(

        text = name,

        modifier = modifier

    )
```

```
}


@Preview(showBackground = true)

@Composable

fun GreetingPreview() {

  MyFirstAppTheme {

    Greeting(stringResource(id = R.string.welcome_message))

  }

}
```

Personal Insight:

The strings.xml file is a great example of how Android separates code from resources. This makes it easier to manage and update your app's content, especially when supporting multiple languages.

Tips and Considerations:

- **Resource Naming:** Use descriptive names for your resources to make them easy to identify.
- **Organization:** Keep your resources organized in appropriate folders.
- **Manifest File:** The AndroidManifest.xml file is crucial for defining your app's components and permissions.

- **Gradle Files:** The build.gradle files are essential for managing dependencies and build configurations.

3.2 Introduction to Gradle and Dependencies: Building Your App's Foundation

Let's talk about Gradle and dependencies, two essential components of Android development. Gradle is the build automation system that handles compiling, packaging, and deploying your app, while dependencies are external libraries that add functionality to your app.

What is Gradle?

Gradle is a powerful build automation system that automates the process of building your Android app. It handles tasks like:

- **Compiling Source Code:** Converts your Kotlin code into executable bytecode.
- **Managing Dependencies:** Downloads and integrates external libraries.
- **Packaging Resources:** Bundles your app's resources (images, layouts, etc.) into an APK or App Bundle.
- **Signing the App:** Digitally signs your app for release.

Why Gradle?

- **Flexibility:** Gradle is highly configurable and can be customized to suit your project's needs.

- **Dependency Management:** It simplifies the process of adding and managing external libraries.
- **Build Automation:** It automates repetitive tasks, saving you time and effort.
- **Consistency:** It ensures consistent builds across different development environments.

Understanding Dependencies

Dependencies are external libraries that provide additional functionality to your app. They can be:

- **Android Jetpack Libraries:** Google-provided libraries that enhance Android development.
- **Third-Party Libraries:** Libraries from other developers that provide specific features.
- **Local Libraries:** Libraries that you create and include in your project.

Gradle Build Files

There are two main build.gradle files in your Android project:

1. **Project-Level** build.gradle:
   - Located in the root directory of your project.
   - Defines build configurations that apply to all modules in your project.
   - Example:
2. Gradle

```
// Top-level build file where you can add configuration options common to all
sub-projects/modules.

plugins {

    id("com.android.application") version "8.2.2" apply false

    id("org.jetbrains.kotlin.android") version "1.9.22" apply false

}
```

3. **Module-Level** build.gradle **(app/build.gradle):**
    o   Located in the app module directory.
    o   Defines build configurations specific to the app module.
    o   Example:
4. Gradle

```
plugins {

    id("com.android.application")

    id("org.jetbrains.kotlin.android")

}


android {

    namespace = "com.example.myfirstapp"
```

```
compileSdk = 34


defaultConfig {

    applicationId = "com.example.myfirstapp"

    minSdk = 24

    targetSdk = 34

    versionCode = 1

    versionName = "1.0"


    testInstrumentationRunner = "androidx.test.runner.AndroidJUnitRunner"

    vectorDrawables {

        useSupportLibrary = true

    }

}


buildTypes {

    release {

        minifyEnabled = false
```

```
            proguardFiles(getDefaultProguardFile("proguard-android-optimize.txt"),
"proguard-rules.pro")

        }

    }

    compileOptions {

        sourceCompatibility = JavaVersion.VERSION_17

        targetCompatibility = JavaVersion.VERSION_17

    }

    kotlinOptions {

        jvmTarget = "17"

    }

    buildFeatures {

        compose = true

    }

    composeOptions {

        kotlinCompilerExtensionVersion = "1.5.1"

    }

    packaging {
```

```
    resources {

        excludes += "/META-INF/{AL2.0,LGPL2.1}"

    }

  }

}


dependencies {


    implementation("androidx.core:core-ktx:1.12.0")

    implementation("androidx.lifecycle:lifecycle-runtime-ktx:2.7.0")

    implementation("androidx.activity:activity-compose:1.8.2")

    implementation(platform("androidx.compose:compose-bom:2024.02.01"))

    implementation("androidx.compose.ui:ui")

    implementation("androidx.compose.ui:ui-graphics")

    implementation("androidx.compose.ui:ui-tooling-preview")

    implementation("androidx.compose.material3:material3")

    testImplementation("junit:junit:4.13.2")

    androidTestImplementation("androidx.test.ext:junit:1.1.5")
```

androidTestImplementation("androidx.test.espresso:espresso-core:3.5.1")

androidTestImplementation(platform("androidx.compose:compose-bom:2024.02.0 1"))

androidTestImplementation("androidx.compose.ui:ui-test-junit4")

debugImplementation("androidx.compose.ui:ui-tooling")

debugImplementation("androidx.compose.ui:ui-test-manifest")

}

Practical Implementation: Adding a Dependency

Let's add the coil-compose library, which simplifies image loading in Compose.

1. **Add the Dependency:**
   - Open your module-level build.gradle file (app/build.gradle).
   - Add the following line to the dependencies block:
2. Gradle

```
dependencies {

   // ... other dependencies

   implementation("io.coil-kt:coil-compose:2.5.0") // Check for latest version

}
```

3. **Sync Gradle Files:**
   - Click the "Sync Project with Gradle Files" button in the toolbar.
4. **Use the Dependency in Compose:**
   - In your Compose code, use the AsyncImage composable from the coil-compose library.
   - Example:
5. Kotlin

```kotlin
import androidx.compose.runtime.Composable

import androidx.compose.ui.tooling.preview.Preview

import coil.compose.AsyncImage


@Composable

fun MyImage() {

  AsyncImage(

    model = "https://via.placeholder.com/150",

    contentDescription = "Example Image"

  )

}
```

```
@Preview(showBackground = true)

@Composable

fun MyImagePreview() {

    MyImage()

}
```

Gradle and dependencies were a bit of a mystery to me at first. But once I understood how they work, they became invaluable tools. They save a lot of time and effort by automating build processes and managing external libraries.

Tips and Considerations:

- **Dependency Versions:** Use stable versions of dependencies to avoid compatibility issues.
- **Gradle Sync:** Always sync your Gradle files after making changes to the build.gradle files.
- **Gradle Plugins:** Explore Gradle plugins to extend its functionality.
- **Dependency Conflicts:** Be aware of dependency conflicts and resolve them if necessary.

Gradle and dependencies are fundamental to Android development.[8] Gradle automates the build process, while dependencies provide additional functionality to your app.[9] By understanding and using these tools effectively, you can build robust and feature-rich Android applications. Remember to keep your dependencies up-to-date and use stable versions to ensure compatibility.

3.3 Understanding the AndroidManifest.xml: Your App's Declaration

Let's talk about the AndroidManifest.xml file, a crucial component of your Android app. Think of it as your app's declaration, providing essential information to the Android system.

What is the AndroidManifest.xml?

The AndroidManifest.xml file is a configuration file that contains metadata about your app. It tells the Android system:

- **App Components:** Activities, services, broadcast receivers, and content providers.
- **Permissions:** What permissions your app requires to access system resources.
- **Hardware and Software Features:** What hardware and software features your app uses.
- **Minimum SDK Version:** The minimum Android version your app supports.
- **App Icon and Label:** The app's icon and label that appear in the launcher.

Why is it Important?

- **System Understanding:** The Android system uses the manifest file to understand your app's requirements and capabilities.

- **Component Registration:** All app components must be declared in the manifest file.
- **Permission Management:** Users are informed about the permissions your app requests.
- **Feature Compatibility:** The system ensures that your app is installed on devices that meet its requirements.

Key Elements

1. <manifest>:
    - The root element of the manifest file.
    - Contains the package name and other global attributes.
2. <application>:
    - Defines the application's components and attributes.
    - Includes the app icon, label, theme, and other settings.
3. <activity>:
    - Defines an activity, which is a single, focused thing that the user can do.
    - Each activity must be declared in the manifest file.
4. <service>:
    - Defines a service, which is a background process that performs long-running operations.
5. <receiver>:
    - Defines a broadcast receiver, which responds to system-wide broadcast announcements.

6. \<provider\>:

   ○ Defines a content provider, which manages shared app data.

7. \<uses-permission\>:

   ○ Declares the permissions your app requires.

8. \<uses-feature\>:

   ○ Declares the hardware and software features your app requires.

9. \<intent-filter\>:

   ○ Defines the intents that an activity, service, or broadcast receiver can handle.

Practical Implementation: Adding a Permission

Let's add the INTERNET permission to your app, which allows it to access the internet.

1. **Open** AndroidManifest.xml:

   ○ In Android Studio, navigate to app/AndroidManifest.xml and open it.

2. **Add the** \<uses-permission\> **Element:**

   ○ Add the following line inside the \<manifest\> element:

3. XML

```
<uses-permission android:name="android.permission.INTERNET" />
```

4. **Complete** AndroidManifest.xml **Example:**

5. XML

```xml
<?xml version="1.0" encoding="utf-8"?>

<manifest xmlns:android="http://schemas.android.com/apk/res/android"

    xmlns:tools="http://schemas.android.com/tools">



    <uses-permission android:name="android.permission.INTERNET" />



    <application

        android:allowBackup="true"

        android:dataExtractionRules="@xml/data_extraction_rules"

        android:icon="@mipmap/ic_launcher"

        android:label="@string/app_name"

        android:roundIcon="@mipmap/ic_launcher_round"

        android:supportsRtl="true"

        android:theme="@style/Theme.MyFirstApp"

        tools:targetApi="31">
```

```xml
        <activity

            android:name=".MainActivity"

            android:exported="true"

            android:label="@string/app_name"

            android:theme="@style/Theme.MyFirstApp">

            <intent-filter>

                <action android:name="android.intent.action.MAIN" />

                <category android:name="android.intent.category.LAUNCHER" />

            </intent-filter>

        </activity>

    </application>


</manifest>
```

Personal Insight:

The AndroidManifest.xml file might seem a bit technical, but it's a crucial part of your app. Getting comfortable with it will give you more control over your app's behavior. I have found it helpful to read the documentation on each element when I am working on a new feature.

Tips and Considerations:

- **Permissions:** Only request the permissions that your app truly needs.
- **Component Declaration:** Always declare your app's components in the manifest file.
- **Intent Filters:** Use intent filters to define how your app responds to intents.
- **Manifest Merging:** Be aware of manifest merging, which combines manifest files from different libraries.
- **Tools Namespace:** The tools namespace is used for development-time attributes.

The AndroidManifest.xml file is a vital component of your Android app. It provides essential information to the Android system and ensures that your app functions correctly. By understanding its key elements and using it effectively, you can build robust and feature-rich Android applications. Remember to keep your manifest file up-to-date and use it to declare your app's components, permissions, and features.

Part 2: Building User Interfaces with Jetpack Compose

Chapter 4: Introduction to Jetpack Compose

Welcome to the exciting world of Jetpack Compose! In this chapter, we'll start building user interfaces using Compose, Android's modern UI toolkit. Get ready to ditch the old XML layouts and embrace a new, declarative way of building UIs.

4.1 Compose Fundamentals: Composables and Modifiers - Building Blocks of Your UI

Let's dive into the core concepts of Jetpack Compose: composables and modifiers. These are the fundamental building blocks that allow you to create beautiful and interactive user interfaces.

Composables: The UI Functions

Composables are functions that describe a piece of your UI. They're annotated with @Composable and are the basic units of UI construction in Compose.

- **What They Are:**
    - Composable functions can emit UI elements, like Text, Button, or Image.
    - They are reusable and composable, meaning you can combine them to create complex UIs.
    - They are declarative, meaning you describe *what* you want the UI to look like, not *how* to build it.
- **Example:**
- Kotlin

```
import androidx.compose.material3.Text

import androidx.compose.runtime.Composable


@Composable

fun Greeting(name: String) {

  Text(text = "Hello, $name!")

}
```

- **Explanation:**
  - The @Composable annotation tells Compose that this function is a UI component.
  - The Greeting function takes a String parameter and displays it in a Text composable.

Modifiers: Customizing Your Composables

Modifiers are used to customize the appearance and behavior of composables. They allow you to add padding, change colors, set sizes, and more.

- **What They Are:**
  - Modifiers are chained together to apply multiple customizations.
  - They are immutable, meaning each modifier returns a new modified instance.

- They are used to add functionality to composables without modifying their core implementation.

- **Example:**
- Kotlin

```kotlin
import androidx.compose.foundation.background

import androidx.compose.foundation.layout.padding

import androidx.compose.material3.Text

import androidx.compose.runtime.Composable

import androidx.compose.ui.Modifier

import androidx.compose.ui.graphics.Color

import androidx.compose.ui.unit.dp


@Composable

fun StyledGreeting(name: String) {

  Text(

    text = "Hello, $name!",

    modifier = Modifier

      .padding(16.dp)
```

```
        .background(Color.LightGray)

    )

}
```

- **Explanation:**
  - The Modifier.padding(16.dp) adds 16 density-independent pixels of padding around the Text.
  - The Modifier.background(Color.LightGray) sets the background color of the Text to light gray.

Practical Implementation: Combining Composables and Modifiers

Let's create a more complex composable that uses multiple modifiers and combines different composables.

Kotlin

```
import androidx.compose.foundation.Image

import androidx.compose.foundation.background

import androidx.compose.foundation.layout.Column

import androidx.compose.foundation.layout.padding

import androidx.compose.foundation.layout.size

import androidx.compose.material3.Text
```

```kotlin
import androidx.compose.runtime.Composable

import androidx.compose.ui.Alignment

import androidx.compose.ui.Modifier

import androidx.compose.ui.graphics.Color

import androidx.compose.ui.res.painterResource

import androidx.compose.ui.unit.dp

import androidx.compose.ui.unit.sp

import com.example.myfirstapp.R // Replace with your R file


@Composable

fun ProfileCard(name: String, description: String) {

    Column(

        modifier = Modifier

            .background(Color.White)

            .padding(16.dp),

        horizontalAlignment = Alignment.CenterHorizontally

    ) {

        Image(
```

```kotlin
        painter = painterResource(id = R.drawable.ic_launcher_foreground), //
Replace with your image resource

        contentDescription = "Profile Picture",

        modifier = Modifier.size(100.dp)

    )

    Text(

        text = name,

        fontSize = 20.sp,

        modifier = Modifier.padding(top = 8.dp)

    )

    Text(

        text = description,

        fontSize = 16.sp,

        modifier = Modifier.padding(top = 4.dp)

    )

    }

}
```

- **Explanation:**
  - The ProfileCard composable uses a Column to arrange the Image and Text vertically.
  - Modifiers are used to add padding, background color, and size.
  - The Image composable uses a painterResource to load an image from the drawable folder.
  - Note: You will need to replace R.drawable.ic_launcher_foreground with your own image resource.

When I first started with Compose, the concept of composables felt a bit strange. But once I realized they were just functions that describe UI, it clicked. Chaining modifiers also felt weird, until I realized how much cleaner it was than XML.

Tips and Considerations:

- **Composable Reusability:** Design composables to be reusable across your app.
- **Modifier Order:** The order of modifiers matters, as they are applied sequentially.
- **Performance:** Avoid unnecessary recompositions by using remember and derivedStateOf.
- **Previews:** Use Android Studio's previews to quickly iterate on your UI.

4.2 Building Basic UI Elements (Text, Buttons, Images): The Core of Your Interface

Let's get hands-on with the essential UI elements in Jetpack Compose: Text, Buttons, and Images. These are the workhorses of your app's interface, allowing you to display information, handle user interactions, and add visual appeal.

Text: Displaying Information

The Text composable is used to display text in your app. It's highly customizable and allows you to control the appearance of your text.

- **Basic Usage:**
- Kotlin
  - import androidx.compose.material3.Text
  - import androidx.compose.runtime.Composable
  - @Composable
  - fun SimpleText() {
  - Text(text = "Hello, Compose!")}

- **Customization:**
- Kotlin
  - import androidx.compose.material3.Text
  - import androidx.compose.runtime.Composable
  - import androidx.compose.ui.graphics.Color
  - import androidx.compose.ui.text.font.FontWeight
  - import androidx.compose.ui.unit.sp
  - @Composable
  - fun StyledText() {

- Text(
- text = "Styled Text",
- color = Color.Blue,
- fontSize = 20.sp,
- fontWeight = FontWeight.Bold
-)
- }

- **Explanation:**
  - You can change the color, fontSize, fontWeight, and other attributes of the text.

Buttons: Handling User Interactions

The Button composable allows users to trigger actions in your app. It's used for interactive elements.

- **Basic Usage:**
- Kotlin

```kotlin
import androidx.compose.material3.Button
import androidx.compose.material3.Text
import androidx.compose.runtime.Composable
@Composable
fun SimpleButton() {
    Button(onClick = {
        // Handle button click
    }) {
```

- Text(text = "Click Me")
- }
- }

- **Customization:**

- Kotlin

  - import androidx.compose.material3.Button
  - import androidx.compose.material3.Text
  - import androidx.compose.runtime.Composable
  - import androidx.compose.ui.Modifier
  - import androidx.compose.ui.graphics.Color
  - import androidx.compose.ui.unit.dp
  - import androidx.compose.foundation.layout.padding

  - @Composable
  - fun StyledButton() {
  -   Button(
  -     onClick = {
  -       // Handle button click
  -     },
  -     modifier = Modifier.padding(16.dp)
  -   ) {
  -     Text(
  -       text = "Styled Button",

- ○   color = Color.White
- ○   )
- ○   }
- ○ }

- **Explanation:**
  - ○ The onClick lambda is executed when the button is clicked.
  - ○ You can customize the button's appearance using modifiers and other attributes.

Images: Adding Visual Appeal

The Image composable is used to display images in your app.

- **Loading from Resources:**
- Kotlin
  - ○ import androidx.compose.foundation.Image
  - ○ import androidx.compose.runtime.Composable
  - ○ import androidx.compose.ui.res.painterResource
  - ○ import com.example.myfirstapp.R // Replace with your R file
  - ○ @Composable
  - ○ fun ResourceImage() {
  - ○   Image(
  - ○   painter = painterResource(id = R.drawable.ic_launcher_foreground), // Replace with your image
  - ○   contentDescription = "My Image")
  - ○ }

- **Loading from URL (using Coil):**

- Kotlin

  - import androidx.compose.foundation.layout.size

  - import androidx.compose.runtime.Composable

  - import androidx.compose.ui.Modifier

  - import androidx.compose.ui.unit.dp

  - import coil.compose.AsyncImage

  - @Composable

  - fun NetworkImage() {

  - AsyncImage(

  - model = "https://via.placeholder.com/150",

  - contentDescription = "Network Image",

  - modifier = Modifier.size(150.dp)

  -)

  - }

- **Explanation:**

  - painterResource loads an image from your drawable folder.

  - AsyncImage (from the Coil library) loads an image from a URL. Remember to add the Coil dependency to your gradle file.

Practical Implementation: Combining Elements

Let's create a simple profile card that combines Text, Button, and Image.

Kotlin

```
import androidx.compose.foundation.Image
import androidx.compose.foundation.layout.Column
import androidx.compose.foundation.layout.padding
import androidx.compose.foundation.layout.size
import androidx.compose.material3.Button
import androidx.compose.material3.Text
import androidx.compose.runtime.Composable
import androidx.compose.ui.Alignment
import androidx.compose.ui.Modifier
import androidx.compose.ui.res.painterResource
import androidx.compose.ui.unit.dp
import androidx.compose.ui.unit.sp
import com.example.myfirstapp.R // Replace with your R file

@Composable
fun ProfileCard() {
    Column(
        modifier = Modifier.padding(16.dp),
        horizontalAlignment = Alignment.CenterHorizontally
    ) {
        Image(
```

```
painter = painterResource(id =
    R.drawable.ic_launcher_foreground), // Replace with your image
        contentDescription = "Profile Picture",
        modifier = Modifier.size(100.dp)
    )
    Text(
        text = "John Doe",
        fontSize = 20.sp,
        modifier = Modifier.padding(top = 8.dp)
    )
    Button(onClick = {
        // Handle button click
    }, modifier = Modifier.padding(top = 16.dp)) {
        Text(text = "Follow")
    }
  }
}
```

These basic UI elements are the foundation of any Android app. Mastering them is essential for creating engaging and user-friendly interfaces. I find it really fun to play with the different attributes and see how they affect the appearance of the elements.

Tips and Considerations:

- **Accessibility:** Ensure your text has sufficient contrast and provide content descriptions for images.

- **User Experience:** Design your buttons to be easily tappable and provide clear feedback on user interactions.

- **Image Optimization:** Optimize your images for different screen densities to reduce app size and improve performance.

- **Coil:** Coil is a very powerful library for image loading, and is highly recommended.

Text, Buttons, and Images are the fundamental UI elements in Jetpack Compose. By understanding how to use and customize them, you can create the building blocks for your app's interface. Remember to prioritize accessibility, user experience, and performance when designing your UI.

4.3 Previewing Your UI in Android Studio: Instant Visual Feedback

Let's explore one of the most powerful features of Jetpack Compose: UI previews. This allows you to see your UI changes in real-time within Android Studio, without needing to run your app on an emulator or device.

Why UI Previews are Essential

UI previews provide instant visual feedback, which is crucial for:

- **Rapid Iteration:** Quickly see the effects of your UI changes without waiting for a build.

- **Design Validation:** Ensure your UI looks as intended on different screen sizes and orientations.

- **Error Detection:** Identify layout issues and visual glitches early in the development process.

- **Improved Workflow:** Streamline your UI development process and increase productivity.

How to Create a Preview

To create a preview, you need to annotate a composable function with @Preview.

- **Basic Preview:**
- Kotlin

```kotlin
import androidx.compose.material3.Text

import androidx.compose.runtime.Composable

import androidx.compose.ui.tooling.preview.Preview


@Composable

fun MyText(text: String) {

    Text(text = text)
```

```
}

@Preview(showBackground = true)

@Composable

fun MyTextPreview() {

    MyText(text = "Hello, Preview!")

}
```

- **Explanation:**
  - The @Preview annotation tells Android Studio to render this composable in the preview pane.
  - showBackground = true adds a background to the preview.
  - The preview function calls the actual composable you want to preview.

Customizing Previews

You can customize previews to simulate different scenarios:

- **Device Configuration:**
- Kotlin

```kotlin
import androidx.compose.ui.tooling.preview.Devices

@Preview(device = Devices.PIXEL_4)

@Composable

fun Pixel4Preview() {

  MyText(text = "Pixel 4 Preview")

}
```

- **Multiple Previews:**
  - Kotlin

```kotlin
@Preview(name = "Light Mode", showBackground = true)

@Preview(name = "Dark Mode", showBackground = true, uiMode =
android.content.res.Configuration.UI_MODE_NIGHT_YES)

@Composable

fun MultiplePreviews() {

  MyText(text = "Multiple Previews")}
```

- **Grouped Previews:**
  - Kotlin

```kotlin
@Preview(group = "Text Previews", name = "Small Text")

@Composable

fun SmallTextPreview() {

  Text(text = "Small")

}



@Preview(group = "Text Previews", name = "Large Text")

@Composable

fun LargeTextPreview() {

  Text(text = "Large")

}
```

- **Explanation:**
  - Devices.PIXEL_4 simulates a Pixel 4 device.
  - uiMode = android.content.res.Configuration.UI_MODE_NIGHT_YES simulates dark mode.
  - group allows you to organize previews.

Practical Implementation: Previewing a Profile Card

Let's preview the ProfileCard composable we created in the previous section.

Kotlin

```kotlin
import androidx.compose.foundation.Image

import androidx.compose.foundation.layout.Column

import androidx.compose.foundation.layout.padding

import androidx.compose.foundation.layout.size

import androidx.compose.material3.Button

import androidx.compose.material3.Text

import androidx.compose.runtime.Composable

import androidx.compose.ui.Alignment

import androidx.compose.ui.Modifier

import androidx.compose.ui.res.painterResource

import androidx.compose.ui.tooling.preview.Preview

import androidx.compose.ui.unit.dp

import androidx.compose.ui.unit.sp

import com.example.myfirstapp.R // Replace with your R file
```

```kotlin
@Composable

fun ProfileCard() {

    // ... (ProfileCard composable from previous example)

    Column(

        modifier = Modifier.padding(16.dp),

        horizontalAlignment = Alignment.CenterHorizontally

    ) {

        Image(

            painter = painterResource(id = R.drawable.ic_launcher_foreground), // Replace with your image

            contentDescription = "Profile Picture",

            modifier = Modifier.size(100.dp)

        )

        Text(

            text = "John Doe",

            fontSize = 20.sp,

            modifier = Modifier.padding(top = 8.dp)

        )
```

```kotlin
    Button(onClick = {

        // Handle button click

    }, modifier = Modifier.padding(top = 16.dp)) {

        Text(text = "Follow")

    }

    }

}


@Preview(showBackground = true)

@Composable

fun ProfileCardPreview() {

    ProfileCard()

}
```

UI previews have significantly improved my development workflow. Being able to see changes instantly saves a lot of time and allows me to focus on the design and functionality of my UI. I highly recommend spending some time getting familiar with all of the preview annotations.

Tips and Considerations:

- **Preview Organization:** Use groups and names to organize your previews.
- **Realistic Data:** Use realistic data in your previews to simulate real-world scenarios.
- **Preview Devices:** Use different device configurations to test your UI on various screen sizes.
- **Interactive Previews:** You can even make previews interactive, though this is a more advanced topic.
- **Performance:** Keep your preview composables lightweight to ensure fast rendering.

UI previews are a powerful tool for Jetpack Compose development. By using previews effectively, you can streamline your workflow, improve your UI design, and catch errors early. Remember to customize your previews to simulate different scenarios and test your UI on various devices.

Chapter 5: Layouts and UI Design

Now that you've got the hang of basic composables, let's dive into creating more complex and visually appealing layouts. This chapter will focus on how to arrange your UI elements and design responsive interfaces using Jetpack Compose.

5.1 Working with Layout Composables (Column, Row, Box): Structuring Your UI

Let's explore the fundamental layout composables in Jetpack Compose: Column, Row, and Box. These are the tools you'll use to arrange and structure your UI elements.

Why Layout Composables?

Layout composables provide the structure for your UI, defining how elements are arranged and positioned. They are essential for creating organized and responsive layouts.

Column: Vertical Arrangement

The Column composable arranges its children vertically, one below the other.

- **Basic Usage:**
- Kotlin

import androidx.compose.foundation.layout.Column

import androidx.compose.material3.Text

```kotlin
import androidx.compose.runtime.Composable

@Composable

fun VerticalLayout() {

    Column {

        Text(text = "Item 1")

        Text(text = "Item 2")

        Text(text = "Item 3")

    }

}
```

- **Customization:**
- Kotlin

```kotlin
import androidx.compose.foundation.layout.Column

import androidx.compose.foundation.layout.fillMaxSize

import androidx.compose.foundation.layout.padding

import androidx.compose.material3.Text

import androidx.compose.runtime.Composable
```

```kotlin
import androidx.compose.ui.Alignment

import androidx.compose.ui.Modifier

import androidx.compose.ui.unit.dp


@Composable

fun StyledColumn() {

    Column(

        modifier = Modifier

            .fillMaxSize()

            .padding(16.dp),

        horizontalAlignment = Alignment.CenterHorizontally

    ) {

        Text(text = "Item 1")

        Text(text = "Item 2")

        Text(text = "Item 3")

    }

}
```

- **Explanation:**

- horizontalAlignment controls the horizontal alignment of the children.
- Modifier.fillMaxSize() makes the column take up the entire screen.
- Modifier.padding(16.dp) adds padding around the column.

Row: Horizontal Arrangement

The Row composable arranges its children horizontally, side by side.

- **Basic Usage:**
- Kotlin

```
import androidx.compose.foundation.layout.Row

import androidx.compose.material3.Text

import androidx.compose.runtime.Composable


@Composable

fun HorizontalLayout() {

  Row {

    Text(text = "Item 1")

    Text(text = "Item 2")

    Text(text = "Item 3")
```

```
        }

}
```

- **Customization:**
- Kotlin

```
import androidx.compose.foundation.layout.Row

import androidx.compose.foundation.layout.padding

import androidx.compose.material3.Text

import androidx.compose.runtime.Composable

import androidx.compose.ui.Alignment

import androidx.compose.ui.Modifier

import androidx.compose.ui.unit.dp


@Composable

fun StyledRow() {

  Row(

    modifier = Modifier.padding(16.dp),

    verticalAlignment = Alignment.CenterVertically
```

```kotlin
) {
    Text(text = "Item 1")

    Text(text = "Item 2")

    Text(text = "Item 3")

}

}
```

- **Explanation:**
    - verticalAlignment controls the vertical alignment of the children.
    - Modifier.padding(16.dp) adds padding around the row.

Box: Stacked Arrangement

The Box composable stacks its children on top of each other. It's useful for overlaying elements.

- **Basic Usage:**
- Kotlin

```kotlin
import androidx.compose.foundation.background

import androidx.compose.foundation.layout.Box

import androidx.compose.foundation.layout.size
```

```kotlin
import androidx.compose.material3.Text

import androidx.compose.runtime.Composable

import androidx.compose.ui.Alignment

import androidx.compose.ui.Modifier

import androidx.compose.ui.graphics.Color

import androidx.compose.ui.unit.dp


@Composable

fun StackedLayout() {

  Box(modifier = Modifier.size(100.dp)) {

    Box(

      modifier = Modifier

        .size(50.dp)

        .background(Color.LightGray)

    )

    Text(

      text = "Overlay",

      modifier = Modifier.align(Alignment.Center)
```

```
    )

  }

}
```

- **Explanation:**
  - Modifier.align(Alignment.Center) aligns the text to the center of the box.
  - The second box, and the text, are placed on top of the first box.

Practical Implementation: Combining Layout Composables

Let's create a simple profile layout using Column, Row, and Box.

```kotlin
Kotlin

import androidx.compose.foundation.Image

import androidx.compose.foundation.layout.Box

import androidx.compose.foundation.layout.Column

import androidx.compose.foundation.layout.Row

import androidx.compose.foundation.layout.padding

import androidx.compose.foundation.layout.size

import androidx.compose.material3.Text

import androidx.compose.runtime.Composable
```

```kotlin
import androidx.compose.ui.Alignment

import androidx.compose.ui.Modifier

import androidx.compose.ui.res.painterResource

import androidx.compose.ui.unit.dp

import androidx.compose.ui.unit.sp

import com.example.myfirstapp.R // Replace with your R file


@Composable

fun ProfileLayout() {

    Column(modifier = Modifier.padding(16.dp)) {

        Box(modifier = Modifier.align(Alignment.CenterHorizontally)) {

            Image(

                painter = painterResource(id = R.drawable.ic_launcher_foreground), //
Replace with your image

                contentDescription = "Profile Picture",

                modifier = Modifier.size(100.dp)

            )

        }
```

```
Text(

    text = "John Doe",

    fontSize = 20.sp,

    modifier = Modifier.align(Alignment.CenterHorizontally)

)

Row(modifier = Modifier.padding(top = 8.dp)) {

    Text(text = "Followers: 100", modifier = Modifier.weight(1f))

    Text(text = "Following: 50", modifier = Modifier.weight(1f))

    }

  }

}
```

- **Explanation:**
  - The Column arranges the profile picture, name, and follower/following counts vertically.
  - The Box is used to center the profile picture.
  - The Row arranges the follower and following counts horizontally.
  - The weight modifier is used to distribute the available space evenly.

Layout composables are the backbone of your UI. Understanding how to use them effectively is crucial for creating well-organized and responsive layouts. I find that sketching out my layouts before coding helps me visualize how to use these composables.

Tips and Considerations:

- **Nesting:** You can nest layout composables to create complex layouts.
- **Modifiers:** Use modifiers to customize the appearance and behavior of your layouts.
- **Alignment:** Use alignment to control the positioning of children within layouts.
- **Weight:** Use the weight modifier to distribute available space among children.
- **Previews:** Use Android Studio's previews to quickly iterate on your layout.

Column, Row, and Box are the fundamental layout composables in Jetpack Compose. By understanding how to use them effectively, you can create organized and responsive UIs. Remember to use modifiers to customize your layouts and use previews to iterate quickly.

5.2 Creating Responsive and Adaptive UIs: Building for Every Screen

Let's talk about creating UIs that look great on any device, regardless of screen size or orientation. Building responsive and adaptive UIs is crucial for providing a seamless user experience.

Why Responsive and Adaptive UIs?

- **Diverse Devices:** Android runs on a wide range of devices, from small phones to large tablets and foldables.
- **User Experience:** Users expect apps to adapt to their device and orientation.
- **Maintainability:** A responsive UI is easier to maintain and update.

Key Concepts

1. **Responsive Design:**
   - Adjusts the layout based on the available screen space.
   - Uses flexible layouts and dynamic sizing.
2. **Adaptive Design:**
   - Adapts the UI based on specific device characteristics, such as screen size or orientation.
   - Uses different layouts or components for different devices.

Techniques for Responsive Design

1. **Using** Modifier.weight():
   - Distributes available space among children in a Row or Column.
   - Example:
2. Kotlin
   - import androidx.compose.foundation.layout.Row
   - import androidx.compose.foundation.layout.fillMaxWidth
   - import androidx.compose.foundation.layout.padding

- import androidx.compose.material3.Text

- import androidx.compose.runtime.Composable

- import androidx.compose.ui.Modifier

- import androidx.compose.ui.unit.dp

-

- @Composable

- fun WeightedRow() {

-    Row(modifier = Modifier.fillMaxWidth().padding(16.dp)) {

-       Text(text = "Left", modifier = Modifier.weight(1f))

-       Text(text = "Right", modifier = Modifier.weight(1f))

-    }

- }

3. **Using** Modifier.fillMaxWidth() **and** Modifier.fillMaxHeight()**:**
   - Makes a composable take up the maximum available width or height.
   - This is very useful inside of a column or row.

4. **Using** Modifier.fillMaxSize()**:**
   - Makes a composable take up the entire available screen.

5. **Using** IntrinsicSize**:**
   - Allows composables to size themselves based on their content.
   - Example:

6. Kotlin
   - import androidx.compose.foundation.layout.Column
   - import androidx.compose.foundation.layout.IntrinsicSize
   - import androidx.compose.foundation.layout.fillMaxWidth
   - import androidx.compose.foundation.layout.padding
   - import androidx.compose.material3.Text
   - import androidx.compose.runtime.Composable

```
o   import androidx.compose.ui.Modifier

o   import androidx.compose.ui.unit.dp

o

o   @Composable

o   fun IntrinsicSizeColumn() {

o       Column(modifier = Modifier.fillMaxWidth().padding(16.dp),

o       modifier =
        Modifier.fillMaxWidth().padding(16.dp).height(IntrinsicSize.Min)) {

o           Text(text = "Short Text")

o           Text(text = "This is a longer text that will determine the height.")

o       }

o   }
```

Techniques for Adaptive Design

1. **Using** Configuration**:**
   - Access device configuration information, such as screen size and orientation.
   - Example:

2. Kotlin
   - import android.content.res.Configuration
   - import androidx.compose.material3.Text
   - import androidx.compose.runtime.Composable
   - import androidx.compose.ui.platform.LocalConfiguration
   -
   - @Composable

```
o   fun OrientationAwareText() {
o       val configuration = LocalConfiguration.current
o       val orientation = configuration.orientation
o
o       val text = if (orientation ==
        Configuration.ORIENTATION_PORTRAIT) {
o           "Portrait Mode"
o       } else {
o           "Landscape Mode"
o       }
o
o       Text(text = text)
o   }
```

3. **Using** WindowSizeClass:

   o Determine the window size class (compact, medium, expanded).
   o This allows for designs that change based on screen size.
   o Add the dependency:

   implementation("androidx.compose.material3:material3-window-size-class:1.2.0-beta01")

   o Example:

4. Kotlin

   o import
   androidx.compose.material3.windowsizeclass.ExperimentalMaterial3WindowSizeClassApi

   o import
   androidx.compose.material3.windowsizeclass.WindowWidthSizeClass

```
import
androidx.compose.material3.windowsizeclass.calculateWindowSizeCl
ass
import androidx.compose.runtime.Composable
import androidx.compose.ui.platform.LocalContext

@OptIn(ExperimentalMaterial3WindowSizeClassApi::class)
@Composable
fun WindowSizeAwareText() {
    val windowSizeClass =
calculateWindowSizeClass(LocalContext.current as
android.app.Activity)
    val widthSizeClass = windowSizeClass.widthSizeClass

    val text = when (widthSizeClass) {
        WindowWidthSizeClass.Compact -> "Compact Width"
        WindowWidthSizeClass.Medium -> "Medium Width"
        WindowWidthSizeClass.Expanded -> "Expanded Width"
        else -> "Unknown Width"
    }

    Text(text = text)
}
```

Practical Implementation: Adaptive Layout

Let's create a layout that adapts to different orientations.

Kotlin

```kotlin
import android.content.res.Configuration
import androidx.compose.foundation.layout.Column
import androidx.compose.foundation.layout.Row
import androidx.compose.foundation.layout.fillMaxSize
import androidx.compose.material3.Text
import androidx.compose.runtime.Composable
import androidx.compose.ui.platform.LocalConfiguration

@Composable
fun AdaptiveLayout() {
    val configuration = LocalConfiguration.current
    val orientation = configuration.orientation

    if (orientation == Configuration.ORIENTATION_PORTRAIT) {
        Column(modifier = androidx.compose.ui.Modifier.fillMaxSize())
    {
            Text(text = "Top Content")
            Text(text = "Bottom Content")
        }
    } else {
        Row(modifier = androidx.compose.ui.Modifier.fillMaxSize()) {
```

- Text(text = "Left Content")
- Text(text = "Right Content")
- }
- }
- }

Building responsive and adaptive UIs requires careful planning and testing. I've found that using the preview tools in Android Studio and testing on a variety of devices is essential. Also, the window size class is an extremely powerful tool that I recommend everyone become familiar with.

Tips and Considerations:

- **Testing:** Test your UI on different devices and orientations.
- **Previews:** Use Android Studio previews to simulate different screen sizes and orientations.
- **Design Guidelines:** Follow Material Design guidelines for adaptive layouts.
- **Performance:** Optimize your layouts for performance on different devices.

Creating responsive and adaptive UIs is essential for providing a great user experience on Android. By using techniques like Modifier.weight(), Configuration, and WindowSizeClass, you can build UIs that adapt to any device. Remember to test your UIs thoroughly and follow design guidelines.

5.3 Applying Material Design 3 Principles: Elevating Your UI with Modern Design

Let's explore Material Design 3 (Material You), Google's latest design system. It's all about creating personalized and adaptable UIs that feel intuitive and modern.

Why Material Design 3?

- **Personalization:** Allows users to customize the look and feel of their apps.
- **Adaptability:** Ensures UIs look great on various devices and screen sizes.
- **Accessibility:** Prioritizes accessibility for all users.
- **Modern Aesthetics:** Provides a fresh and contemporary look.

Key Principles of Material Design 3

1. **Dynamic Color:**
   - Generates a color palette based on the user's wallpaper.
   - Creates a personalized and cohesive look.

2. **Typography:**
   - Uses a system of type scales for consistent and readable text.
   - Provides clear visual hierarchy.

3. **Shape:**
   - Uses rounded corners and distinct shapes to create visual interest.
   - Provides visual cues for interactive elements.

4. **Elevation:**
   - Uses shadows and elevation to create a sense of depth.
   - Provides visual feedback for interactions.

5. **Components:**
   - ○ Provides a set of pre-designed UI components that follow Material Design 3 principles.
   - ○ Simplifies UI development.

Implementing Material Design 3 in Compose

1. **Setting Up Material Theme:**
   - ○ Compose provides the MaterialTheme composable to apply Material Design 3 styles.
   - ○ Example:
2. Kotlin

```kotlin
import androidx.compose.material3.MaterialTheme

import androidx.compose.material3.Surface

import androidx.compose.runtime.Composable


@Composable

fun MyMaterialApp(content: @Composable () -> Unit) {

MaterialTheme {

    Surface {
```

```
        content()

    }

  }

}
```

3. **Using Material Components:**
   - ○ Compose provides a wide range of Material components, such as Button, Card, and TextField.
   - ○ Example:
4. Kotlin

```
import androidx.compose.material3.Button

import androidx.compose.material3.Text

import androidx.compose.runtime.Composable


@Composable

fun MyMaterialButton() {

  Button(onClick = { /* Handle click */ }) {

    Text(text = "Click Me")

  }
```

}

5. **Applying Dynamic Color:**
   - Material 3 handles dynamic color automatically, as long as you use the MaterialTheme composable.

6. **Customizing Typography:**
   - You can customize the typography of your app by modifying the Typography object in MaterialTheme.
   - Example:

7. Kotlin

```kotlin
import androidx.compose.material3.MaterialTheme

import androidx.compose.material3.Text

import androidx.compose.runtime.Composable

import androidx.compose.ui.text.font.FontWeight

import androidx.compose.ui.unit.sp


@Composable

fun MyStyledText() {

Text(

    text = "Styled Text",
```

```
        style = MaterialTheme.typography.headlineMedium.copy(

            fontWeight = FontWeight.Bold,

            fontSize = 24.sp

        )

    )

}
```

8. **Using Shapes and Elevation:**
    - Material components automatically apply shapes and elevation.
    - You can customize them using the shape and elevation parameters.
    - Example:
9. Kotlin


```kotlin
import androidx.compose.foundation.layout.padding

import androidx.compose.material3.Card

import androidx.compose.material3.Text

import androidx.compose.runtime.Composable

import androidx.compose.ui.Modifier

import androidx.compose.ui.unit.dp
```

```kotlin
@Composable

fun MyElevatedCard() {

    Card(modifier = Modifier.padding(16.dp)) {

        Text(text = "Elevated Card", modifier = Modifier.padding(16.dp))

    }

}
```

Practical Implementation: Applying Material Design 3 to a Profile Card

Let's enhance the profile card from previous examples with Material Design 3.

Kotlin

```kotlin
import androidx.compose.foundation.Image

import androidx.compose.foundation.layout.Column

import androidx.compose.foundation.layout.padding

import androidx.compose.foundation.layout.size

import androidx.compose.material3.Button

import androidx.compose.material3.Card

import androidx.compose.material3.MaterialTheme

import androidx.compose.material3.Text

import androidx.compose.runtime.Composable
```

```kotlin
import androidx.compose.ui.Alignment

import androidx.compose.ui.Modifier

import androidx.compose.ui.res.painterResource

import androidx.compose.ui.unit.dp

import androidx.compose.ui.unit.sp

import com.example.myfirstapp.R // Replace with your R file


@Composable

fun MaterialProfileCard() {

    Card(modifier = Modifier.padding(16.dp)) {

        Column(

            modifier = Modifier.padding(16.dp),

            horizontalAlignment = Alignment.CenterHorizontally

        ) {

            Image(

                painter = painterResource(id = R.drawable.ic_launcher_foreground), // Replace with your image

                contentDescription = "Profile Picture",
```

```kotlin
        modifier = Modifier.size(100.dp)
    )

    Text(

        text = "John Doe",

        style = MaterialTheme.typography.headlineSmall,

        modifier = Modifier.padding(top = 8.dp)

    )

    Button(onClick = {

        // Handle button click

    }, modifier = Modifier.padding(top = 16.dp)) {

        Text(text = "Follow")

    }

        }

    }

}
```

Material Design 3 has made it easier than ever to create beautiful and consistent UIs. The dynamic color feature is particularly impressive, as it adds a touch of personalization that users appreciate. Using the material components is a huge time saver.

Tips and Considerations:

- **Design Guidelines:** Familiarize yourself with the Material Design 3 guidelines.

- **Theming:** Customize the Material Theme to match your app's brand.

- **Accessibility:** Ensure your UI is accessible to all users.

- **Component Usage:** Use Material components whenever possible to ensure consistency.

- **Testing:** Test your UI on different devices and in different color modes.

Chapter 6: Handling User Interactions

Now that you've built some basic layouts, it's time to make them interactive. In this chapter, we'll explore how to handle user events, collect input, and manage the state of your UI.

6.1 Responding to User Events (Button Clicks, Gestures): Making Your App Interactive

Let's dive into the heart of user interaction: handling events like button clicks and gestures. This is where your app comes to life, responding to user actions and providing feedback.

Why Event Handling is Crucial

- **User Engagement:** Makes your app interactive and responsive.
- **Functionality:** Triggers actions and updates based on user input.
- **Usability:** Provides clear feedback and enhances the user experience.

Handling Button Clicks

The most common user event is a button click. Compose makes it easy to handle these events.

- **Basic Button Click:**
- Kotlin

```kotlin
import androidx.compose.material3.Button

import androidx.compose.material3.Text

import androidx.compose.runtime.Composable

import androidx.compose.runtime.mutableStateOf

import androidx.compose.runtime.remember

import androidx.compose.runtime.getValue

import androidx.compose.runtime.setValue


@Composable

fun ClickCounterButton() {

    var clickCount by remember { mutableStateOf(0) }


    Button(onClick = {

      clickCount++

    }) {

      Text(text = "Clicked $clickCount times")

    }

}
```

- **Explanation:**
  - The onClick lambda is executed when the button is clicked.
  - remember { mutableStateOf(0) } creates a state variable that stores the click count.
  - clickCount++ increments the click count.
  - The Text composable displays the updated click count.

Handling Gestures

Compose provides modifiers for handling various gestures, such as taps, swipes, and long presses.

- **Handling Taps:**
- Kotlin

```
import androidx.compose.foundation.clickable

import androidx.compose.material3.Text

import androidx.compose.runtime.Composable

import androidx.compose.ui.Modifier


@Composable

fun TappableText() {
```

```kotlin
Text(

    text = "Tap Me",

    modifier = Modifier.clickable {

        // Handle tap event

    }

)

}
```

- **Handling Long Presses:**
- Kotlin

```kotlin
import androidx.compose.foundation.gestures.detectTapGestures

import androidx.compose.material3.Text

import androidx.compose.runtime.Composable

import androidx.compose.ui.Modifier

import androidx.compose.ui.input.pointer.pointerInput


@Composable

fun LongPressableText() {
```

```
Text(

    text = "Long Press Me",

    modifier = Modifier.pointerInput(Unit) {

        detectTapGestures(

            onLongPress = {

                // Handle long press event

            }

        )

    }

    )

}
```

- **Explanation:**
  - Modifier.clickable handles tap events.
  - Modifier.pointerInput(Unit) { detectTapGestures(onLongPress = { ... }) } handles long press events.
  - detectTapGestures allows you to handle various tap-related gestures.

Practical Implementation: Combining Events and State

Let's create a simple toggle button that changes its text when clicked.

Kotlin

```kotlin
import androidx.compose.material3.Button

import androidx.compose.material3.Text

import androidx.compose.runtime.Composable

import androidx.compose.runtime.mutableStateOf

import androidx.compose.runtime.remember

import androidx.compose.runtime.getValue

import androidx.compose.runtime.setValue


@Composable

fun ToggleButton() {

    var isToggled by remember { mutableStateOf(false) }


    Button(onClick = {

        isToggled = !isToggled

    }) {

        Text(text = if (isToggled) "Toggled On" else "Toggled Off")

    }
```

}

- **Explanation:**
  - isToggled is a state variable that stores the toggle state.
  - The onClick lambda toggles the state.
  - The Text composable displays the appropriate text based on the state.

Handling user events is what makes an app feel alive. When I first started with Android development, event handling seemed complex. But Compose simplifies it significantly. I have learned to use the debugger to make sure that the events are being fired when they are expected.

Tips and Considerations:

- **State Management:** Use state variables to store and update UI data.
- **Lambda Expressions:** Use lambda expressions for concise event handling.
- **Gesture Detection:** Explore detectTapGestures and other gesture modifiers.
- **Accessibility:** Ensure your event handling is accessible to all users.
- **Feedback:** Provide clear feedback to users when events occur.

Responding to user events is essential for creating interactive and engaging Android apps. By using Compose's event handling capabilities, you can build apps that respond to user actions and provide a seamless user experience. Remember to use state management to update your UI and provide clear feedback to users.

6.2 Collecting User Input (TextFields): Gathering Data from Users

Let's explore how to collect user input using TextFields in Jetpack Compose. This is a fundamental part of building interactive forms and gathering data from your users.

Why Collecting User Input is Essential

- **Data Gathering:** Allows users to enter information, such as names, emails, and passwords.
- **Form Submission:** Enables users to submit forms and complete actions.
- **Search Functionality:** Provides a way for users to search for content.
- **User Customization:** Allows users to customize app settings.

Basic TextField Usage

The TextField composable is used to collect user input.

- **Basic TextField:**
- Kotlin
- import androidx.compose.material3.TextField
- import androidx.compose.runtime.Composable
- import androidx.compose.runtime.mutableStateOf
- import androidx.compose.runtime.remember
- import androidx.compose.runtime.getValue
- import androidx.compose.runtime.setValue
-

- @Composable
- fun BasicTextField() {
- var text by remember { mutableStateOf("") }
-
- TextField(
- value = text,
- onValueChange = { text = it },
- label = { androidx.compose.material3.Text("Enter text") }
-)
- }
- **Explanation:**
  - value holds the current text in the TextField.
  - onValueChange is a lambda that is called whenever the text changes.
  - label provides a label for the TextField.
  - remember { mutableStateOf("") } creates a state variable to store the text.

Customizing TextFields

You can customize TextFields to suit your needs.

- **Password TextField:**
- Kotlin
- import androidx.compose.material3.TextField
- import androidx.compose.material3.Text
- import androidx.compose.runtime.Composable

- import androidx.compose.runtime.mutableStateOf

- import androidx.compose.runtime.remember

- import androidx.compose.runtime.getValue

- import androidx.compose.runtime.setValue

- import androidx.compose.ui.text.input.PasswordVisualTransformation

- import androidx.compose.ui.text.input.VisualTransformation

-

- @Composable

- fun PasswordTextField() {

-     var password by remember { mutableStateOf("") }

-

-     TextField(

-         value = password,

-         onValueChange = { password = it },

-         label = { Text("Enter password") },

-         visualTransformation = PasswordVisualTransformation()

-     )

- }

- **Explanation:**
    - PasswordVisualTransformation() hides the entered text.

- **Single Line TextField:**

- Kotlin

- import androidx.compose.material3.TextField

- import androidx.compose.material3.Text

- import androidx.compose.runtime.Composable

- import androidx.compose.runtime.mutableStateOf

- import androidx.compose.runtime.remember

```kotlin
import androidx.compose.runtime.getValue

import androidx.compose.runtime.setValue

import androidx.compose.ui.text.input.ImeAction

import androidx.compose.ui.text.input.KeyboardType


@Composable

fun SingleLineTextField() {

    var text by remember { mutableStateOf("") }


    TextField(

        value = text,

        onValueChange = { text = it },

        label = { Text("Enter text") },

        singleLine = true,

        keyboardOptions =
androidx.compose.ui.text.input.KeyboardOptions(keyboardType =
KeyboardType.Text, imeAction = ImeAction.Done)

    )

}
```

- **Explanation:**
  - singleLine = true makes the TextField a single line.
  - keyboardOptions allows you to customize the keyboard type and IME action.

Practical Implementation: Form with TextFields

Let's create a simple form with TextFields for name and email.

Kotlin

```kotlin
import androidx.compose.foundation.layout.Column
import androidx.compose.foundation.layout.padding
import androidx.compose.material3.Button
import androidx.compose.material3.Text
import androidx.compose.material3.TextField
import androidx.compose.runtime.Composable
import androidx.compose.runtime.mutableStateOf
import androidx.compose.runtime.remember
import androidx.compose.runtime.getValue
import androidx.compose.runtime.setValue
import androidx.compose.ui.Modifier
import androidx.compose.ui.unit.dp

@Composable
fun UserForm() {
    var name by remember { mutableStateOf("") }
    var email by remember { mutableStateOf("") }

    Column(modifier = Modifier.padding(16.dp)) {
        TextField(
            value = name,
            onValueChange = { name = it },
```

- label = { Text("Name") },
- modifier = Modifier.padding(bottom = 8.dp)
-)
- TextField(
- value = email,
- onValueChange = { email = it },
- label = { Text("Email") },
- modifier = Modifier.padding(bottom = 16.dp)
-)
- Button(onClick = {
- // Handle form submission
- }) {
- Text("Submit")
- }
- }
- }

- **Explanation:**
  - The Column arranges the TextFields and Button vertically.
  - State variables store the name and email.
  - The Button's onClick lambda handles form submission.

TextFields are a fundamental part of user interaction. I've found that providing clear labels and visual cues helps users understand what information is expected. I also recommend spending some time becoming familiar with all of the KeyboardOptions.

Tips and Considerations:

- **State Management:** Use state variables to store and update input values.
- **Validation:** Validate user input to ensure it's in the correct format.
- **Accessibility:** Ensure your TextFields are accessible to all users.
- **Keyboard Options:** Customize the keyboard type and IME action for different input types.
- **Visual Transformation:** Use VisualTransformation to hide or transform input values.

Collecting user input using TextFields is essential for building interactive Android apps. By understanding how to use and customize TextFields, you can gather data from users and create engaging experiences. Remember to prioritize state management, validation, and accessibility.

6.3 Managing UI State: Keeping Your UI Consistent and Responsive

Let's talk about UI state management, a crucial aspect of building robust and maintainable Android apps with Jetpack Compose. UI state refers to the data that your UI displays and interacts with. Proper state management ensures your UI remains consistent and responsive to user actions.

Why State Management is Essential

- **Consistency:** Keeps your UI in sync with the underlying data.
- **Reactivity:** Updates the UI when the data changes.
- **Maintainability:** Makes your code easier to understand and debug.

- **Performance:** Prevents unnecessary recompositions.

Key Concepts

1. **State:**
   - Data that can change over time and affect the UI.
   - Examples: user input, loading state, and data from a network request.

2. **Recomposition:**
   - Compose's process of redrawing the UI when the state changes.
   - Only the parts of the UI that depend on the changed state are recomposed.

3. **State Hoisting:**
   - Moving state up to a higher level in the composable hierarchy.
   - Makes the state more manageable and reusable.

State Holders and remember

- remember:
  - A composable function that preserves state across recompositions.
  - Used to create state variables within a composable.
- mutableStateOf:
  - Creates a mutable state object that can be updated.
- Example:
- Kotlin

```kotlin
import androidx.compose.runtime.Composable

import androidx.compose.runtime.mutableStateOf

import androidx.compose.runtime.remember

import androidx.compose.runtime.getValue

import androidx.compose.runtime.setValue

import androidx.compose.material3.Text


@Composable

fun Counter() {

    var count by remember { mutableStateOf(0) }


    androidx.compose.material3.Button(onClick = { count++ }) {

        Text("Count: $count")

    }

}
```

- Explanation:
  - count is a state variable that stores the counter value.
  - remember ensures that the count variable is preserved across recompositions.

- mutableStateOf(0) initializes the count variable to 0.

State Hoisting Example

- Let's create a composable that displays a message and allows the user to change it.
- Kotlin

```
import androidx.compose.material3.TextField

import androidx.compose.runtime.Composable

import androidx.compose.runtime.mutableStateOf

import androidx.compose.runtime.remember

import androidx.compose.runtime.getValue

import androidx.compose.runtime.setValue


@Composable

fun MessageInput() {

    var message by remember { mutableStateOf("") }

    MessageDisplay(message = message, onMessageChange = { message = it })
```

```
}

@Composable

fun MessageDisplay(message: String, onMessageChange: (String) -> Unit) {

    TextField(

        value = message,

        onValueChange = onMessageChange,

        label = { androidx.compose.material3.Text("Enter Message") }

    )

    androidx.compose.material3.Text("Message: $message")

}
```

- Explanation:
  - The MessageInput composable holds the message state.
  - The MessageDisplay composable receives the message and onMessageChange as parameters.
  - State hoisting allows the MessageDisplay composable to be reused with different state sources.

Using ViewModel for Complex State

- For complex state management, especially when dealing with data from network requests or databases, use a ViewModel.
- Kotlin

```kotlin
import androidx.lifecycle.ViewModel

import androidx.compose.runtime.mutableStateOf

import androidx.compose.runtime.getValue

import androidx.compose.runtime.setValue


class MyViewModel : ViewModel() {

    var data by mutableStateOf("Initial Data")

        private set


    fun updateData(newData: String) {

        data = newData

    }

}
```

- Explanation:
  - The ViewModel holds the data state.
  - The updateData function updates the data state.
  - You would then use this viewmodel within your composable.

Practical Implementation: State Management in a Todo List

Let's create a simple todo list with state management.

Kotlin

```kotlin
import androidx.compose.foundation.layout.Column

import androidx.compose.foundation.layout.Row

import androidx.compose.foundation.layout.padding

import androidx.compose.material3.Button

import androidx.compose.material3.Checkbox

import androidx.compose.material3.Text

import androidx.compose.material3.TextField

import androidx.compose.runtime.Composable

import androidx.compose.runtime.mutableStateOf

import androidx.compose.runtime.remember

import androidx.compose.runtime.getValue
```

```kotlin
import androidx.compose.runtime.setValue

import androidx.compose.ui.Alignment

import androidx.compose.ui.Modifier

import androidx.compose.ui.unit.dp


data class TodoItem(val text: String, var isChecked: Boolean = false)


@Composable

fun TodoList() {

    var todoItems by remember { mutableStateOf(mutableListOf<TodoItem>()) }

    var newTodoText by remember { mutableStateOf("") }


    Column(modifier = Modifier.padding(16.dp)) {

        Row(verticalAlignment = Alignment.CenterVertically) {

            TextField(

                value = newTodoText,

                onValueChange = { newTodoText = it },

                label = { Text("New Todo") },
```

```kotlin
            modifier = Modifier.weight(1f)

        )

        Button(onClick = {

            if (newTodoText.isNotEmpty()) {

                todoItems.add(TodoItem(newTodoText))

                newTodoText = ""

            }

        }) {

            Text("Add")

        }

    }

    todoItems.forEachIndexed { index, item ->

        Row(verticalAlignment = Alignment.CenterVertically) {

            Checkbox(

                checked = item.isChecked,

                onCheckedChange = { todoItems[index] = item.copy(isChecked = it)

    }

            )
```

```
            Text(text = item.text)

        }

    }

  }

}
```

State management is a fundamental aspect of building robust and maintainable UIs.I have learned that properly hoisting state makes my composables more reusable and testable. Also, ViewModels are extremely useful for complex state.

Tips and Considerations:

- **State Hoisting:** Hoist state to a common ancestor when multiple composables need to access it.
- remember: Use remember to preserve state across recompositions.
- ViewModel: Use ViewModel for complex state and data management.
- **Immutability:** Use immutable data classes to represent state.
- **Testing:** Write unit tests to verify your state management logic.

Managing UI state is essential for building consistent and responsive Android apps with Jetpack Compose. By using state holders, state hoisting, and ViewModel, you can create robust and maintainable UIs. Remember to prioritize state management and write unit tests to verify your logic.

Part 3: Adding Functionality and Data Management

Chapter 7: Navigation Between Screens

Now that we've covered building UIs and handling user interactions, let's explore how to navigate between different screens within your app. In this chapter, we'll use Navigation Compose, a powerful library for managing navigation in Compose apps.

7.1 Implementing Navigation with Navigation Compose: Guiding Users Through Your App

Let's talk about navigation in Jetpack Compose. Navigation is the backbone of any multi-screen app, allowing users to move seamlessly between different parts of your application. Navigation Compose is Google's recommended way to implement navigation in Compose apps.

Why Navigation Compose?

- **Declarative Navigation:** Aligns with Compose's declarative UI paradigm.
- **Type Safety:** Provides type-safe navigation between screens.
- **Back Stack Management:** Automatically handles the back stack.
- **Deep Linking:** Supports deep linking to specific destinations.
- **Animation Support:** Allows for smooth transitions between screens.

Setting Up Navigation Compose

1. **Add Dependencies:**
   - Add the following dependencies to your module-level build.gradle file:

2. Gradle

dependencies {

   implementation("androidx.navigation:navigation-compose:2.7.7") // Check for latest version

}

3. **Create a** NavHost**:**
    o The NavHost composable is the container for your navigation graph.
4. Kotlin

```kotlin
import androidx.compose.runtime.Composable

import androidx.navigation.compose.NavHost

import androidx.navigation.compose.composable

import androidx.navigation.compose.rememberNavController


@Composable

fun MyAppNavigation() {

   val navController = rememberNavController()

   NavHost(navController = navController, startDestination = "screen1") {
```

```kotlin
        composable("screen1") { Screen1(navController) }

        composable("screen2") { Screen2(navController) }

    }

}
```

- **Explanation:**
  - rememberNavController() creates a NavController that manages the navigation state.
  - NavHost defines the navigation graph, with startDestination specifying the initial screen.
  - composable defines a destination and its associated composable.

Creating Screens

- Create composable functions for each screen in your app.
- Kotlin

```kotlin
import androidx.compose.material3.Button

import androidx.compose.material3.Text

import androidx.compose.runtime.Composable

import androidx.navigation.NavController
```

```kotlin
@Composable

fun Screen1(navController: NavController) {

    androidx.compose.foundation.layout.Column {

        Text("Screen 1")

        Button(onClick = { navController.navigate("screen2") }) {

            Text("Go to Screen 2")

        }

    }

}


@Composable

fun Screen2(navController: NavController) {

    androidx.compose.foundation.layout.Column {

        Text("Screen 2")

        Button(onClick = { navController.popBackStack() }) {

            Text("Go Back")

        }

    }
```

```
}
```

- **Explanation:**
  - navController.navigate("screen2") navigates to "screen2".
  - navController.popBackStack() navigates back to the previous screen.

Passing Arguments

- You can pass arguments between screens using navigation arguments.
- Kotlin

```kotlin
import androidx.compose.material3.Button

import androidx.compose.material3.Text

import androidx.compose.runtime.Composable

import androidx.navigation.NavController

import androidx.navigation.NavType

import androidx.navigation.compose.NavHost

import androidx.navigation.compose.composable

import androidx.navigation.compose.rememberNavController

import androidx.navigation.navArgument
```

```kotlin
@Composable

fun MyAppNavigationWithArgs() {

    val navController = rememberNavController()

    NavHost(navController = navController, startDestination = "screen1") {

        composable("screen1") {

            androidx.compose.foundation.layout.Column {

                Text("Screen 1")

                Button(onClick = { navController.navigate("screen2/John") }) {

                    Text("Go to Screen 2 with argument")

                }

            }

        }

        composable(

            "screen2/{name}",

            arguments = listOf(navArgument("name") { type = NavType.StringType })

        ) { backStackEntry ->
```

```
        Screen2WithArg(navController,

backStackEntry.arguments?.getString("name"))

        }

    }

}


@Composable

fun Screen2WithArg(navController: NavController, name: String?) {

    androidx.compose.foundation.layout.Column {

        Text("Screen 2, Name: $name")

        Button(onClick = { navController.popBackStack() }) {

            Text("Go Back")

        }

    }

}
```

- **Explanation:**
  - composable("screen2/{name}", arguments = ...) defines a destination with a name argument.

- backStackEntry.arguments?.getString("name") retrieves the argument value.

Practical Implementation: Navigation in a Simple App

Let's create a simple app with two screens and navigation.

Kotlin

```kotlin
import androidx.compose.material3.Button

import androidx.compose.material3.Text

import androidx.compose.runtime.Composable

import androidx.navigation.NavController

import androidx.navigation.compose.NavHost

import androidx.navigation.compose.composable

import androidx.navigation.compose.rememberNavController


@Composable

fun SimpleNavigationApp() {

    val navController = rememberNavController()

    NavHost(navController = navController, startDestination = "home") {
```

```kotlin
        composable("home") { HomeScreen(navController) }

        composable("details") { DetailsScreen(navController) }

    }

}


@Composable

fun HomeScreen(navController: NavController) {

    androidx.compose.foundation.layout.Column {

        Text("Home Screen")

        Button(onClick = { navController.navigate("details") }) {

            Text("Go to Details")

        }

    }

}


@Composable

fun DetailsScreen(navController: NavController) {

    androidx.compose.foundation.layout.Column {
```

```
Text("Details Screen")

Button(onClick = { navController.popBackStack() }) {

    Text("Go Back")

    }

  }

}
```

Navigation Compose has simplified navigation in Compose apps. The declarative approach feels natural and makes it easy to manage navigation logic. It is very important to spend time planning your navigation graph.

Tips and Considerations:

- **Navigation Graph:** Plan your navigation graph carefully.
- **Arguments:** Use navigation arguments to pass data between screens.
- **Back Stack:** Understand how the back stack works.
- **Deep Linking:** Implement deep linking for a better user experience.
- **Animations:** Use animations for smooth transitions.

Navigation Compose provides a powerful and flexible way to implement navigation in Jetpack Compose apps. By using NavHost, composable, and navigation arguments, you can create seamless navigation experiences for your users. Remember to plan your navigation graph and use animations for smooth transitions.

7.2 Passing Data Between Screens: Sharing Information in Your App

Let's explore how to pass data between screens in Jetpack Compose using Navigation Compose. This is essential for creating dynamic and interactive apps where information needs to be shared across different parts of your UI.

Why Passing Data is Important

- **Dynamic Content:** Displays content based on user actions or data from previous screens.
- **Contextual Information:** Provides relevant information to users in different parts of your app.
- **Data Sharing:** Allows different screens to share and update data.

Methods for Passing Data

1. **Navigation Arguments:**
   o Used for simple data types (strings, integers, etc.).
   o Passed directly in the navigation route.
2. **ViewModel Sharing:**
   o Used for complex data or state that needs to be shared across multiple screens.
   o Uses a shared ViewModel instance.
3. **Saved State Handle:**
   o Used to pass data that survives process death.

- Useful for preserving state across configuration changes or app restarts.

Passing Data Using Navigation Arguments

- **Defining the Route with Arguments:**
- Kotlin

```
import androidx.navigation.NavType

import androidx.navigation.navArgument

composable(

    "details/{itemId}",

    arguments = listOf(navArgument("itemId") { type = NavType.IntType })

) { backStackEntry ->

    val itemId = backStackEntry.arguments?.getInt("itemId")

    DetailsScreen(itemId)

}
```

- **Navigating with Arguments:**

- Kotlin

```kotlin
navController.navigate("details/123")
```

-
-
- **Retrieving Arguments in the Destination Screen:**
- Kotlin

```kotlin
import androidx.compose.material3.Text

import androidx.compose.runtime.Composable


@Composable

fun DetailsScreen(itemId: Int?) {

    Text("Details for Item ID: $itemId")

}
```

- **Explanation:**
  - The route "details/{itemId}" defines a placeholder for the itemId.
  - navArgument specifies the type of the argument.
  - backStackEntry.arguments?.getInt("itemId") retrieves the argument value.

Passing Data Using ViewModel Sharing

- **Creating a Shared ViewModel:**
- Kotlin

```kotlin
import androidx.lifecycle.ViewModel

import androidx.compose.runtime.mutableStateOf

import androidx.compose.runtime.getValue

import androidx.compose.runtime.setValue


class SharedViewModel : ViewModel() {

    var sharedData by mutableStateOf("Initial Data")

        private set


    fun updateData(newData: String) {

        sharedData = newData

    }

}
```

- **Sharing the ViewModel Instance:**
- Kotlin

```kotlin
import androidx.compose.runtime.Composable

import androidx.lifecycle.viewmodel.compose.viewModel


@Composable

fun ScreenA() {

    val viewModel: SharedViewModel = viewModel()

    androidx.compose.material3.Button(onClick = { viewModel.updateData("New Data from A") }) {

        androidx.compose.material3.Text("Update Shared Data")

    }

}


@Composable

fun ScreenB() {

    val viewModel: SharedViewModel = viewModel()

    androidx.compose.material3.Text("Shared Data: ${viewModel.sharedData}")
```

```
}
```

- **Explanation:**
  - viewModel() retrieves the same instance of SharedViewModel in both screens.
  - Changes made in one screen are reflected in the other.

Practical Implementation: Passing Data in a Product Details App

Let's create a simple product details app with navigation and data passing.

```kotlin
Kotlin

import androidx.compose.material3.Button

import androidx.compose.material3.Text

import androidx.compose.runtime.Composable

import androidx.navigation.NavController

import androidx.navigation.NavType

import androidx.navigation.compose.NavHost

import androidx.navigation.compose.composable

import androidx.navigation.compose.rememberNavController

import androidx.navigation.navArgument
```

```kotlin
data class Product(val id: Int, val name: String)


val products = listOf(

    Product(1, "Laptop"),

    Product(2, "Smartphone"),

    Product(3, "Tablet")

)



@Composable

fun ProductListScreen(navController: NavController) {

    androidx.compose.foundation.layout.Column {

        products.forEach { product ->

            Button(onClick = { navController.navigate("details/${product.id}") }) {

                Text(product.name)

            }

        }

    }

}
```

```kotlin
@Composable

fun ProductDetailsScreen(productId: Int?) {

    val product = products.find { it.id == productId }

    product?.let {

        Text("Product Details: ${it.name}")

    } ?: Text("Product not found")

}


@Composable

fun ProductNavigationApp() {

    val navController = rememberNavController()

    NavHost(navController = navController, startDestination = "list") {

        composable("list") { ProductListScreen(navController) }

        composable(

            "details/{productId}",

            arguments = listOf(navArgument("productId") { type = NavType.IntType
})
```

```
) { backStackEntry ->

    val productId = backStackEntry.arguments?.getInt("productId")

    ProductDetailsScreen(productId)

  }

 }

}
```

Passing data between screens is a fundamental aspect of building dynamic apps. I've found that choosing the right method (navigation arguments, ViewModel sharing, or Saved State Handle) depends on the complexity and scope of the data. ViewModels are extremely useful for sharing data across many screens.

Tips and Considerations:

- **Data Types:** Choose the appropriate data type for your arguments.
- **ViewModel Scope:** Use the correct scope for your ViewModel (activity, fragment, or navigation graph).
- **Saved State Handle:** Use SavedStateHandle for data that needs to survive process death.
- **Testing:** Write unit tests to verify your data passing logic.
- **Error Handling:** Handle cases where arguments are missing or invalid.

Passing data between screens is essential for creating dynamic and interactive Android apps. By using navigation arguments, ViewModel sharing, and Saved State Handle, you can share information across different parts of your UI. Remember to choose the appropriate method based on your needs and write tests to verify your logic.

Chapter 8: Data Persistence

In this chapter, we'll explore how to store and manage data in your Android apps. Data persistence is crucial for creating apps that retain information even after they're closed or the device is restarted.

8.1 Storing Simple Data with Shared Preferences: Persisting User Preferences

Let's explore how to store simple data using Shared Preferences in Android. This is a lightweight mechanism for persisting key-value pairs, ideal for storing user preferences and small amounts of data.

Why Shared Preferences?

- **Simple Storage:** Easy to use for storing basic data types.
- **Lightweight:** Doesn't require a database or complex setup.
- **Persistent:** Data survives app restarts and configuration changes.
- **User Preferences:** Perfect for storing user settings, like theme choices or login status.

How Shared Preferences Works

Shared Preferences stores data in an XML file within the app's private storage. It's best suited for storing simple data types like booleans, integers, floats, and strings.

Implementing Shared Preferences

1. **Get Shared Preferences Instance:**
   - Use context.getSharedPreferences() to get a SharedPreferences instance.
2. Kotlin

```
import android.content.Context

import android.content.SharedPreferences


fun getPrefs(context: Context): SharedPreferences {

    return context.getSharedPreferences("my_prefs", Context.MODE_PRIVATE)

}
```

   - "my_prefs" is the name of the preferences file.
   - Context.MODE_PRIVATE ensures that the preferences file is only accessible by your app.
3. **Storing Data:**
   - Use an SharedPreferences.Editor to modify the preferences.
4. Kotlin

```
fun saveString(context: Context, key: String, value: String) {
```

```
val editor = getPrefs(context).edit()

editor.putString(key, value)

editor.apply() // or editor.commit()

}
```

```
fun saveBoolean(context: Context, key: String, value: Boolean) {

    val editor = getPrefs(context).edit()

    editor.putBoolean(key, value)

    editor.apply()

}
```

- o editor.apply() saves the changes asynchronously.
- o editor.commit() saves the changes synchronously (blocking the UI thread). apply() is generally preferred.

5. **Retrieving Data:**
    - o Use the appropriate get method to retrieve data.

6. Kotlin

```
fun getString(context: Context, key: String, defaultValue: String = ""): String {

    return getPrefs(context).getString(key, defaultValue) ?: defaultValue
```

```kotlin
}
```

```kotlin
fun getBoolean(context: Context, key: String, defaultValue: Boolean = false):
Boolean {

    return getPrefs(context).getBoolean(key, defaultValue)

}
```

- o defaultValue is returned if the key doesn't exist.

Practical Implementation: Storing Theme Preferences

Let's create a simple app that stores the user's theme preference (light or dark).

```kotlin
Kotlin

import android.content.Context

import androidx.compose.material3.Button

import androidx.compose.material3.Text

import androidx.compose.runtime.Composable

import androidx.compose.runtime.mutableStateOf

import androidx.compose.runtime.remember

import androidx.compose.runtime.getValue
```

```kotlin
import androidx.compose.runtime.setValue

import androidx.compose.ui.platform.LocalContext


@Composable

fun ThemePreferenceScreen() {

    val context = LocalContext.current

    var isDarkMode by remember { mutableStateOf(getBoolean(context,
"dark_mode")) }


    androidx.compose.foundation.layout.Column {

        Text(if (isDarkMode) "Dark Mode" else "Light Mode")

        Button(onClick = {

            isDarkMode = !isDarkMode

            saveBoolean(context, "dark_mode", isDarkMode)

        }) {

            Text("Toggle Theme")

        }

    }
```

```
}
```

// Shared Preferences functions from above

- **Explanation:**
  - ○ LocalContext.current provides the current Context.
  - ○ getBoolean(context, "dark_mode") retrieves the theme preference.
  - ○ saveBoolean(context, "dark_mode", isDarkMode) stores the updated preference.

Shared Preferences is a quick and easy way to store simple data. However, it's not suitable for large or complex data sets. I've found that using apply() instead of commit() improves performance by avoiding UI thread blocking. Also, when using shared preferences, it is important to have a clear naming convention for your keys.

Tips and Considerations:

- **Data Types:** Use Shared Preferences for simple data types only.
- apply() **vs.** commit(): Prefer apply() for asynchronous saving.
- **Key Naming:** Use descriptive and consistent key names.
- **Data Security:** Avoid storing sensitive data in Shared Preferences.
- **Alternatives:** Consider using DataStore or Room for more complex data storage.
- **Testing:** Write unit tests to verify your Shared Preferences logic.

Shared Preferences is a valuable tool for storing simple data in Android apps. By understanding how to use it effectively, you can persist user preferences and improve the user experience. Remember to use apply() for asynchronous saving and consider alternatives for more complex data storage.

8.2 Introduction to ViewModel and StateFlow: Modern State Management

Let's dive into two powerful tools for managing UI state in Android: ViewModel and StateFlow. These are key components of modern Android development, especially when working with Jetpack Compose.

Why ViewModel and StateFlow?

- **ViewModel:**
  - Survives configuration changes (like screen rotation).
  - Stores and manages UI-related data in a lifecycle-conscious way.
  - Separates UI logic from UI presentation.
- **StateFlow:**
  - A cold flow that emits the current state and any updates to it.
  - Part of Kotlin Coroutines, providing a reactive way to handle state.
  - Integrates seamlessly with Jetpack Compose.

ViewModel: Lifecycle-Aware Data Holder

The ViewModel class is designed to store and manage UI-related data in a lifecycle-conscious way.

- **Creating a ViewModel:**
  - Kotlin

```kotlin
import androidx.lifecycle.ViewModel


class MyViewModel : ViewModel() {

    // UI-related data and logic

}
```

- **Using ViewModel in Compose:**
  - Kotlin

```kotlin
import androidx.compose.runtime.Composable

import androidx.lifecycle.viewmodel.compose.viewModel


@Composable

fun MyScreen() {

    val viewModel: MyViewModel = viewModel()

    // Access viewModel data and functions

}
```

- **Explanation:**
  - viewModel() retrieves or creates an instance of the ViewModel.
  - The ViewModel survives configuration changes.

StateFlow: Reactive State Management

StateFlow is a cold flow that holds a current state value and emits updates to that value.

- **Adding Dependency:**
  - Ensure your project has the coroutines dependencies.
- **Creating a StateFlow:**
- Kotlin

```
import kotlinx.coroutines.flow.MutableStateFlow

import kotlinx.coroutines.flow.StateFlow


class MyViewModel : ViewModel() {

  private val _myState = MutableStateFlow("Initial State")

  val myState: StateFlow<String> = _myState


  fun updateState(newState: String) {
```

```
    _myState.value = newState

  }

}
```

- **Explanation:**
  - MutableStateFlow is used to create a mutable state.
  - StateFlow is a read-only interface.
  - _myState.value updates the state.
- **Collecting StateFlow in Compose:**
- Kotlin

```
import androidx.compose.runtime.Composable

import androidx.compose.runtime.collectAsState

import androidx.compose.runtime.getValue

import androidx.lifecycle.viewmodel.compose.viewModel

@Composable

fun MyScreen() {

  val viewModel: MyViewModel = viewModel()

  val state by viewModel.myState.collectAsState()
```

```
androidx.compose.material3.Text(state)
```

}

- **Explanation:**
  - collectAsState() collects the StateFlow and converts it to a Compose state.
  - Whenever the StateFlow emits a new value, the UI is recomposed.

Practical Implementation: Combining ViewModel and StateFlow

Let's create a simple counter app using ViewModel and StateFlow.

```kotlin
Kotlin

import androidx.compose.material3.Button

import androidx.compose.material3.Text

import androidx.compose.runtime.Composable

import androidx.compose.runtime.collectAsState

import androidx.compose.runtime.getValue

import androidx.lifecycle.ViewModel

import androidx.lifecycle.viewmodel.compose.viewModel

import kotlinx.coroutines.flow.MutableStateFlow

import kotlinx.coroutines.flow.StateFlow
```

```kotlin
class CounterViewModel : ViewModel() {

    private val _count = MutableStateFlow(0)

    val count: StateFlow<Int> = _count


    fun increment() {

        _count.value++

    }

}



@Composable

fun CounterScreen() {

    val viewModel: CounterViewModel = viewModel()

    val count by viewModel.count.collectAsState()


    androidx.compose.foundation.layout.Column {

        Text("Count: $count")

        Button(onClick = { viewModel.increment() }) {
```

```
        Text("Increment")

    }

  }

}
```

- **Explanation:**
  - CounterViewModel manages the counter state.
  - _count is a MutableStateFlow that holds the counter value.
  - CounterScreen collects the count state and updates the UI.

ViewModel and StateFlow have become essential tools in my Android development. The combination of lifecycle-aware data storage and reactive state updates makes building complex UIs much more manageable. Especially with compose. I have found the debugging Stateflow and viewmodels to be quite effective.

Tips and Considerations:

- **State Management:** Use StateFlow for UI state that changes over time.
- **ViewModel Scope:** Understand the scope of your ViewModel.
- **Flow Operators:** Use flow operators to transform and manipulate state.
- **Testing:** Write unit tests for your ViewModel and flow logic.
- **MutableStateFlow vs. StateFlow**: always expose stateflow, and manipulate MutableStateflow internally inside of the viewmodel.

ViewModel and StateFlow are powerful tools for managing UI state in Android. By using them effectively, you can create robust, maintainable, and responsive apps. Remember to use ViewModel for lifecycle-aware data storage and StateFlow for reactive state updates.

8.3 Displaying Lists with Compose: Efficiently Rendering Data

Let's explore how to display lists efficiently in Jetpack Compose. Lists are a fundamental part of many apps, and Compose provides powerful tools to render them smoothly and performantly.

Why Lists are Important

- **Data Display:** Shows collections of data to the user.
- **User Interaction:** Enables users to interact with items in a list.
- **Efficient Rendering:** Optimizes performance for large datasets.

Key Composables for Lists

1. LazyColumn:
   - Vertically scrolling list that only composes and lays out visible items.
   - Efficient for large lists.
2. LazyRow:
   - Horizontally scrolling list that only composes and lays out visible items.
   - Efficient for horizontal lists.

3. items:

   ○ A scope function used inside LazyColumn and LazyRow to iterate and display list items.

Using LazyColumn

- **Basic Usage:**
- Kotlin

```
import androidx.compose.foundation.lazy.LazyColumn

import androidx.compose.foundation.lazy.items

import androidx.compose.material3.Text

import androidx.compose.runtime.Composable


@Composable

fun MyList(items: List<String>) {

  LazyColumn {

    items(items) { item ->
```

```kotlin
        Text(text = item)

    }

  }

}
```

- **Explanation:**
  - LazyColumn creates a vertically scrolling list.
  - items(items) iterates over the list and creates a composable for each item.
  - Text(text = item) displays each item.
- **Adding Item Keys:**
  - Use items(items, key = { item -> item.id }) to provide a unique key for each item.
  - Improves performance when items are added, removed, or reordered.
- Kotlin

```kotlin
data class MyItem(val id: Int, val text: String)


@Composable

fun MyListWithKeys(items: List<MyItem>) {

  LazyColumn {

    items(items, key = { item -> item.id }) { item ->
```

```
    Text(text = item.text)

    }

  }

}
```

Using LazyRow

- **Basic Usage:**
- Kotlin

```kotlin
import androidx.compose.foundation.lazy.LazyRow

import androidx.compose.foundation.lazy.items

import androidx.compose.material3.Text

import androidx.compose.runtime.Composable


@Composable

fun MyHorizontalList(items: List<String>) {

  LazyRow {

    items(items) { item ->

      Text(text = item)
```

```
        }

    }

}
```

- **Explanation:**
  - LazyRow creates a horizontally scrolling list.
  - The rest works the same way as LazyColumn.

Practical Implementation: Displaying a List of Products

Let's create a simple product list using LazyColumn.

Kotlin

```kotlin
import androidx.compose.foundation.layout.Column

import androidx.compose.foundation.layout.padding

import androidx.compose.foundation.lazy.LazyColumn

import androidx.compose.foundation.lazy.items

import androidx.compose.material3.Card

import androidx.compose.material3.Text

import androidx.compose.runtime.Composable

import androidx.compose.ui.Modifier
```

```kotlin
import androidx.compose.ui.unit.dp

data class Product(val id: Int, val name: String, val price: Double)

val products = listOf(

    Product(1, "Laptop", 1200.0),

    Product(2, "Smartphone", 800.0),

    Product(3, "Tablet", 500.0),

    Product(4, "Headphones", 150.0),

    Product(5, "Smartwatch", 300.0)

)


@Composable

fun ProductList() {

    LazyColumn(modifier = Modifier.padding(16.dp)) {

        items(products, key = { product -> product.id }) { product ->

            ProductItem(product = product)

        }
```

```kotlin
    }

}


@Composable

fun ProductItem(product: Product) {

    Card(modifier = Modifier.padding(8.dp)) {

        Column(modifier = Modifier.padding(16.dp)) {

            Text(text = product.name)

            Text(text = "Price: $${product.price}")

        }

    }

}
```

- **Explanation:**
  - LazyColumn displays the list of products.
  - items(products, key = { product -> product.id }) iterates over the products and provides a unique key.
  - ProductItem displays the product details.

LazyColumn and LazyRow have significantly improved the performance of list rendering in Compose. The lazy loading mechanism ensures that only visible items are composed, which is crucial for large datasets. I highly recommend always using item keys to improve performance.

Tips and Considerations:

- **Item Keys:** Always provide unique keys for items to improve performance.
- **Lazy Loading:** Use LazyColumn and LazyRow for efficient list rendering.
- **Item Layout:** Design efficient item layouts to avoid performance issues.
- **Scroll State:** Use rememberLazyListState() to control the scroll position.
- **Animations:** Add animations for item insertion, removal, and reordering.
- **Performance:** Test your lists with large datasets to ensure smooth scrolling.

Displaying lists efficiently is crucial for building performant Android apps. By using LazyColumn and LazyRow, you can create smooth and responsive lists. Remember to provide item keys and design efficient item layouts.

Chapter 9: Networking and APIs

In this chapter, we'll explore how to fetch data from the internet using networking and APIs. This is a crucial skill for building apps that display dynamic content and interact with online services.

9.1 Making Simple Network Requests: Connecting Your App to the Web

Let's explore how to make simple network requests in Android. This is crucial for fetching data from the internet, like weather updates, news articles, or user information.

Why Network Requests?

- **Data Retrieval:** Fetches dynamic data from web services.
- **API Integration:** Enables your app to interact with external APIs.
- **Real-time Updates:** Provides users with up-to-date information.

Key Concepts and Tools

1. **HTTP (Hypertext Transfer Protocol):**
   - The foundation of data communication on the web.
   - Uses methods like GET, POST, PUT, and DELETE.
2. **Kotlin Coroutines:**
   - A concurrency design pattern for simplifying asynchronous code.
   - Crucial for making network requests without blocking the UI thread.

3. **Retrofit:**

   - A type-safe HTTP client for Android and Java.

   - Simplifies the process of making network requests.

   - Uses annotations to define API endpoints.

4. **Gson (Google JSON):**

   - A Java library that can be used to convert Java Objects into their JSON representation.

   - A JSON library to convert JSON to Java objects and vice-versa.

Setting Up Dependencies

1. **Retrofit and Gson:**

   - Add the following dependencies to your module-level build.gradle file:

2. Gradle

```
dependencies {

    implementation("com.squareup.retrofit2:retrofit:2.9.0") // Check for latest version

    implementation("com.squareup.retrofit2:converter-gson:2.9.0")
```

```
implementation("com.squareup.okhttp3:logging-interceptor:4.9.3") // Optional,
for logging

}
```

3. **Internet Permission:**
   - o Add the following permission to your AndroidManifest.xml file:
4. XML

```xml
<uses-permission android:name="android.permission.INTERNET" />
```

Implementing Network Requests with Retrofit

1. **Define Data Classes:**
   - o Create data classes to represent the JSON response.
2. Kotlin

```kotlin
data class Post(val userId: Int, val id: Int, val title: String, val body: String)
```

3. **Create an API Interface:**
   - o Define the API endpoints using Retrofit annotations.
4. Kotlin

```kotlin
import retrofit2.http.GET

import retrofit2.http.Path
```

```kotlin
import retrofit2.http.Query

interface ApiService {

    @GET("posts")

    suspend fun getPosts(): List<Post>


    @GET("posts/{id}")

    suspend fun getPost(@Path("id") id: Int): Post


    @GET("comments")

    suspend fun getComments(@Query("postId") postId: Int): List<Comment>


}

data class Comment(val postId: Int, val id: Int, val name: String, val email: String,
val body: String)
```

5. **Create a Retrofit Instance:**
   - Build a Retrofit instance using a base URL.
6. Kotlin

```kotlin
import retrofit2.Retrofit

import retrofit2.converter.gson.GsonConverterFactory

import okhttp3.OkHttpClient

import okhttp3.logging.HttpLoggingInterceptor


object RetrofitClient {

    private const val BASE_URL = "https://jsonplaceholder.typicode.com/"


    private val loggingInterceptor = HttpLoggingInterceptor().apply {

        level = HttpLoggingInterceptor.Level.BODY // Log request and response
body

    }


    private val okHttpClient = OkHttpClient.Builder()

        .addInterceptor(loggingInterceptor)

        .build()


    val apiService: ApiService by lazy {
```

```
Retrofit.Builder()

    .baseUrl(BASE_URL)

    .addConverterFactory(GsonConverterFactory.create())

    .client(okHttpClient)

    .build()

    .create(ApiService::class.java)

  }

}
```

7. Make Network Requests in a Coroutine:

  o Use viewModelScope.launch to make network requests in a coroutine.

8. Kotlin

```
import androidx.lifecycle.ViewModel

import androidx.lifecycle.viewModelScope

import kotlinx.coroutines.launch

import kotlinx.coroutines.flow.MutableStateFlow

import kotlinx.coroutines.flow.StateFlow
```

```kotlin
class MainViewModel : ViewModel() {

    private val _posts = MutableStateFlow<List<Post>>(emptyList())

    val posts: StateFlow<List<Post>> = _posts


    fun fetchPosts() {

        viewModelScope.launch {

            try {

                val posts = RetrofitClient.apiService.getPosts()

                _posts.value = posts

            } catch (e: Exception) {

                // Handle error

                println("Error fetching posts: ${e.message}")

            }

        }

    }

}
```

9. **Display Data in Compose:**
    o Collect the StateFlow and display the data.

```kotlin
import androidx.compose.material3.Text

import androidx.compose.runtime.Composable

import androidx.compose.runtime.collectAsState

import androidx.compose.runtime.getValue

import androidx.lifecycle.viewmodel.compose.viewModel


@Composable

fun PostListScreen() {

    val viewModel: MainViewModel = viewModel()

    val posts by viewModel.posts.collectAsState()


    androidx.compose.foundation.lazy.LazyColumn {

        items(posts) { post ->

            Text(text = post.title)

        }

    }
```

}

Retrofit has significantly simplified network requests in Android. The declarative approach with annotations makes it easy to define API endpoints. Using coroutines ensures that network requests are performed asynchronously, preventing UI thread blocking. Always remember to handle potential exceptions when making network requests.

Tips and Considerations:

- **Error Handling:** Implement robust error handling for network requests.
- **Loading States:** Display loading indicators while fetching data.
- **Caching:** Cache network responses to improve performance.
- **Authentication:** Implement authentication for protected APIs.
- **Testing:** Write unit tests for your API service and ViewModel.
- **Logging:** Use logging interceptors to debug network requests.

9.2 Displaying Data from APIs: Bringing Web Content to Your App

Let's explore how to display data fetched from APIs in your Android app using Jetpack Compose. This is where your app transforms from a static interface to a dynamic, data-driven experience.

Why Displaying API Data is Essential

- **Dynamic Content:** Provides users with real-time, up-to-date information.
- **Feature Enrichment:** Enhances app functionality by integrating with external services.

- **User Engagement:** Keeps users engaged with fresh and relevant content.

Key Steps and Considerations

1. **Fetching Data:**
   - Use Retrofit and Kotlin Coroutines (as covered in 9.1) to fetch data from the API.
2. **State Management:**
   - Use ViewModel and StateFlow to manage the API data and loading states.
3. **UI Rendering:**
   - Use Jetpack Compose to display the fetched data in a user-friendly way.
4. **Error Handling:**
   - Implement robust error handling to gracefully handle network errors or API failures.
5. **Loading Indicators:**
   - Provide visual feedback to users while data is being fetched.

Practical Implementation: Displaying a List of Users from an API

Let's build an app that fetches a list of users from a public API (e.g., JSONPlaceholder) and displays them in a LazyColumn.

1. **Data Classes:**
2. Kotlin

```kotlin
data class User(

    val id: Int,

    val name: String,

    val email: String,

    val username: String

)
```

3. **API Interface (ApiService):**
4. Kotlin

```kotlin
import retrofit2.http.GET


interface ApiService {

    @GET("users")

    suspend fun getUsers(): List<User>

}
```

5. **Retrofit Client (RetrofitClient):**
6. Kotlin

```kotlin
import retrofit2.Retrofit

import retrofit2.converter.gson.GsonConverterFactory

import okhttp3.OkHttpClient

import okhttp3.logging.HttpLoggingInterceptor


object RetrofitClient {

    private const val BASE_URL = "https://jsonplaceholder.typicode.com/"


    private val loggingInterceptor = HttpLoggingInterceptor().apply {

        level = HttpLoggingInterceptor.Level.BODY

    }


    private val okHttpClient = OkHttpClient.Builder()

        .addInterceptor(loggingInterceptor)

        .build()


    val apiService: ApiService by lazy {

        Retrofit.Builder()
```

```
            .baseUrl(BASE_URL)

            .addConverterFactory(GsonConverterFactory.create())

            .client(okHttpClient)

            .build()

            .create(ApiService::class.java)

    }

}
```

7. **ViewModel (UserViewModel):**
8. Kotlin

```kotlin
import androidx.lifecycle.ViewModel

import androidx.lifecycle.viewModelScope

import kotlinx.coroutines.flow.MutableStateFlow

import kotlinx.coroutines.flow.StateFlow

import kotlinx.coroutines.launch


class UserViewModel : ViewModel() {

    private val _users = MutableStateFlow<List<User>>(emptyList())
```

```kotlin
val users: StateFlow<List<User>> = _users

private val _isLoading = MutableStateFlow(false)

val isLoading: StateFlow<Boolean> = _isLoading

private val _errorMessage = MutableStateFlow<String?>(null)

val errorMessage: StateFlow<String?> = _errorMessage

init {

    fetchUsers()

}

fun fetchUsers() {

    viewModelScope.launch {

        _isLoading.value = true

        _errorMessage.value = null

        try {

            val users = RetrofitClient.apiService.getUsers()
```

```kotlin
            _users.value = users

        } catch (e: Exception) {

            _errorMessage.value = "Failed to fetch users: ${e.message}"

        } finally {

            _isLoading.value = false

        }

    }

}
```

9. **Compose UI (UserListScreen):**
10. Kotlin

```kotlin
import androidx.compose.foundation.layout.Box

import androidx.compose.foundation.layout.Column

import androidx.compose.foundation.layout.fillMaxSize

import androidx.compose.foundation.layout.padding

import androidx.compose.foundation.lazy.LazyColumn

import androidx.compose.foundation.lazy.items
```

```kotlin
import androidx.compose.material3.CircularProgressIndicator

import androidx.compose.material3.Text

import androidx.compose.runtime.Composable

import androidx.compose.runtime.collectAsState

import androidx.compose.runtime.getValue

import androidx.compose.ui.Alignment

import androidx.compose.ui.Modifier

import androidx.compose.ui.unit.dp

import androidx.lifecycle.viewmodel.compose.viewModel


@Composable

fun UserListScreen() {

    val viewModel: UserViewModel = viewModel()

    val users by viewModel.users.collectAsState()

    val isLoading by viewModel.isLoading.collectAsState()

    val errorMessage by viewModel.errorMessage.collectAsState()


    Box(modifier = Modifier.fillMaxSize()) {
```

```kotlin
    if (isLoading) {

        CircularProgressIndicator(modifier = Modifier.align(Alignment.Center))

    } else if (errorMessage != null) {

        Text(text = errorMessage!!, modifier = Modifier.align(Alignment.Center))

    } else {

        LazyColumn(modifier = Modifier.padding(16.dp)) {

            items(users) { user ->

                UserItem(user = user)

            }

        }

    }

}


@Composable

fun UserItem(user: User) {

    Column(modifier = Modifier.padding(8.dp)) {

        Text(text = user.name)
```

```
        Text(text = user.email)

        Text(text = user.username)


    }


}
```

Displaying API data is what makes apps truly dynamic. I've found that using StateFlow to manage loading and error states significantly improves the user experience. Always remember to provide clear visual feedback to users when data is being fetched or when errors occur.

Tips and Considerations:

- **Loading States:** Use CircularProgressIndicator or other loading indicators.
- **Error Handling:** Display user-friendly error messages.
- **Caching:** Implement caching to reduce network requests.
- **Data Transformation:** Transform API data into a format suitable for your UI.
- **Testing:** Write integration tests to verify API data display.
- **UI/UX:** Design your UI to handle various data states (loading, empty, error, success).

Displaying data from APIs is a core part of modern Android development. By using Retrofit, Kotlin Coroutines, ViewModel, and Jetpack Compose, you can create dynamic and engaging apps. Remember to handle errors, provide loading indicators, and design user-friendly UIs.

Part 4: Testing, Debugging, and Publishing

Chapter 10: Debugging and Testing

In this chapter, we'll explore how to debug and test your Android apps. Debugging is the process of finding and fixing errors in your code, while testing ensures that your app behaves as expected.

10.1 Using Android Studio Debugging Tools: Unraveling the Mysteries of Your Code

Let's talk about debugging in Android Studio. Debugging is an essential skill for any developer, allowing you to identify and fix issues in your code efficiently. Android Studio provides a powerful set of debugging tools to help you do just that.

Why Debugging Tools Are Essential

- **Error Detection:** Pinpoints the source of bugs and crashes.
- **Code Understanding:** Helps you understand how your code executes step by step.
- **Performance Analysis:** Identifies performance bottlenecks.
- **Efficiency:** Saves time and effort in fixing issues.

Key Debugging Tools in Android Studio

1. **Breakpoints:**
   o Pauses the execution of your code at a specific line.
   o Allows you to inspect variables and step through your code.
2. **Debugger Window:**
   o Displays the current state of variables, call stack, and threads.

- Provides controls for stepping through code.

3. **Logcat:**
   - Displays system and application logs.
   - Helps you track down errors and monitor application behavior.

4. **Variable Inspection:**
   - Allows you to examine the values of variables at runtime.

5. **Step Over, Step Into, Step Out:**
   - Controls for stepping through code execution.

Using Breakpoints and the Debugger Window

1. **Setting a Breakpoint:**
   - Click in the gutter (the area to the left of the line numbers) next to the line of code where you want to pause execution.

2. **Running in Debug Mode:**
   - Click the "Debug" button (the bug icon) in the toolbar.

3. **Inspecting Variables:**
   - When the breakpoint is hit, the debugger window will appear.
   - You can inspect the values of variables in the "Variables" pane.

4. **Stepping Through Code:**
   - Use the following buttons in the debugger window:
     - **Step Over (F8):** Executes the current line and moves to the next line in the same function.
     - **Step Into (F7):** Steps into the function call on the current line.
     - **Step Out (Shift + F8):** Steps out of the current function and returns to the calling function.

- **Resume Program (F9):** Continues execution until the next breakpoint or the end of the program.

Using Logcat

1. **Opening Logcat:**
   - Click the "Logcat" tab at the bottom of Android Studio.
2. **Filtering Logs:**
   - Use the filter options to narrow down the logs:
     - **Log Level:** Select the log level (e.g., Verbose, Debug, Info, Warn, Error).
     - **Tag:** Filter logs by tag (e.g., a custom tag you added in your code).
     - **Package Name:** Filter logs by your app's package name.
     - Search bar: filter by search terms.
3. **Adding Log Messages:**
   - Use Log methods in your code to add log messages.
4. Kotlin

```kotlin
import android.util.Log

fun myFunction() {
    val myVariable = 10
```

```
Log.d("MyTag", "myVariable: $myVariable")

// ...

}
```

Practical Implementation: Debugging a Simple Counter

Let's debug a simple counter app to demonstrate breakpoints and Logcat.

1. **Create a Simple Counter App:**
2. Kotlin

```
import androidx.compose.material3.Button

import androidx.compose.material3.Text

import androidx.compose.runtime.Composable

import androidx.compose.runtime.mutableStateOf

import androidx.compose.runtime.remember

import androidx.compose.runtime.getValue

import androidx.compose.runtime.setValue

import android.util.Log


@Composable
```

```kotlin
fun CounterScreen() {

    var count by remember { mutableStateOf(0) }


    androidx.compose.foundation.layout.Column {

        Text("Count: $count")

        Button(onClick = {

            count++

            Log.d("CounterTag", "Count incremented to: $count")

        }) {

            Text("Increment")

        }

    }

}
```

3. **Set a Breakpoint:**
   - Set a breakpoint on the line count++.

4. **Run in Debug Mode:**
   - Click the "Debug" button.

5. **Inspect Variables:**
   - When the breakpoint is hit, inspect the value of count in the debugger window.

6. **Step Through Code:**
   - Use "Step Over" to move to the next line.
7. **Check Logcat:**
   - Open Logcat and filter by "CounterTag" to see the log messages.

Debugging is an essential skill that saves a lot of time and frustration. I've found that using breakpoints and stepping through code is particularly helpful for understanding complex logic. Logcat is invaluable for tracking down errors and monitoring application behavior. I recommend everyone become very comfortable with these tools.

Tips and Considerations:

- **Use Breakpoints Strategically:** Set breakpoints where you suspect issues might occur.
- **Inspect Variables Carefully:** Pay attention to the values of variables to understand the state of your application.
- **Use Logcat Effectively:** Filter logs to find relevant information.
- **Test Edge Cases:** Debug your code with different input values to test edge cases.
- **Learn Keyboard Shortcuts:** Use keyboard shortcuts to speed up your debugging workflow.
- **Remote Debugging:** Android studio also supports remote debugging, in case you need to debug a device that is not directly connected to your computer.

Android Studio's debugging tools are essential for identifying and fixing issues in your code. By using breakpoints, the debugger window, and Logcat, you can efficiently debug your Android apps. Remember to use these tools strategically and practice regularly to improve your debugging skills.

10.2 Testing on Emulators and Physical Devices: Ensuring Your App Works Everywhere

Let's s talk about testing your Android apps on emulators and physical devices. Thorough testing is critical for ensuring your app works flawlessly on a wide range of devices and configurations.

Why Testing on Both Emulators and Physical Devices?

- **Emulators:**
    - Convenient for rapid testing during development.
    - Allows you to simulate various device configurations.
    - Useful for testing edge cases and different API levels.
- **Physical Devices:**
    - Provides a realistic user experience.
    - Tests hardware-specific features (camera, sensors, etc.).
    - Helps identify performance issues on real hardware.

Testing on Emulators

1. **Creating an Emulator:**

   ○ Open the AVD (Android Virtual Device) Manager in Android Studio (Tools > AVD Manager).

   ○ Click "Create Virtual Device."

   ○ Select a device definition (e.g., Pixel 7).

   ○ Choose a system image (API level).

   ○ Configure any advanced settings (optional).

   ○ Click "Finish."

2. **Running Your App on an Emulator:**

   ○ Select the emulator from the device dropdown in the toolbar.

   ○ Click the "Run" button (the green triangle).

3. **Emulator Features:**

   ○ **Rotation:** Simulate device rotation.

   ○ **Network Speed:** Simulate different network conditions.

   ○ **GPS:** Simulate GPS location.

   ○ **Battery:** Simulate battery level and charging.

   ○ **Camera:** Simulate camera input.

Testing on Physical Devices

1. **Enabling USB Debugging:**

   ○ On your Android device, go to Settings > About Phone.

   ○ Tap "Build number" seven times to enable Developer options.

   ○ Go to Settings > Developer options.

o Enable "USB debugging."

2. **Connecting the Device:**

   o Connect your device to your computer using a USB cable.

   o Allow USB debugging on your device when prompted.

3. **Running Your App on a Physical Device:**

   o Select your device from the device dropdown in the toolbar.

   o Click the "Run" button.

4. **Testing Hardware Features:**

   o Test hardware-specific features like the camera, sensors, and GPS.

   o Test performance on real hardware.

   o Test interactions with real-world conditions.

Practical Implementation: Testing a Camera Feature

Let's assume you have a simple app with a camera feature.

1. **Emulator Testing:**

   o Create an emulator with camera support.

   o Run your app and test the camera functionality using the emulator's simulated camera.

2. **Physical Device Testing:**

   o Connect a physical device with a camera.

   o Run your app and test the camera functionality using the device's camera.

   o Test in different lighting conditions and with different subjects.

3. **Code Example (Simplified Camera Intent):**

4. Kotlin

```kotlin
import android.content.Intent

import android.provider.MediaStore

import androidx.activity.compose.rememberLauncherForActivityResult

import androidx.activity.result.contract.ActivityResultContracts

import androidx.compose.material3.Button

import androidx.compose.material3.Text

import androidx.compose.runtime.Composable


@Composable

fun CameraButton() {

    val cameraLauncher = rememberLauncherForActivityResult(

        contract = ActivityResultContracts.StartActivityForResult()

    ) { result ->

        // Handle result (e.g., display the captured image)
```

```
    }


    Button(onClick = {

        val cameraIntent = Intent(MediaStore.ACTION_IMAGE_CAPTURE)

        cameraLauncher.launch(cameraIntent)

    }) {

        Text("Take Photo")

    }

}
```

Testing on both emulators and physical devices is crucial for delivering a high-quality app. I've found that emulators are excellent for rapid testing and simulating various configurations, while physical devices are essential for testing hardware-specific features and performance. I recommend testing on a wide range of real devices to catch device-specific issues.

Tips and Considerations:

- **Test on Multiple Devices:** Test on a variety of devices with different screen sizes, resolutions, and API levels.
- **Test on Different Android Versions:** Test on different Android versions to ensure compatibility.
- **Test in Different Network Conditions:** Test on different network speeds and connection types.

- **Test in Different Orientations:** Test in both portrait and landscape orientations.

- **Test Hardware Features:** Test hardware-specific features like the camera, sensors, and GPS.

- **Use Testing Tools:** Use Android Studio's testing tools (e.g., Espresso, JUnit) for automated testing.

- **Consider Beta Testing:** Release a beta version of your app to a small group of users for real-world testing.

- **Cloud Testing:** use services like Firebase Test Lab to test your application on a wide variety of devices.

Testing on both emulators and physical devices is essential for ensuring your Android app works flawlessly. By using emulators for rapid testing and physical devices for realistic testing, you can deliver a high-quality app to your users. Remember to test on a wide range of devices and configurations to catch device-specific issues.

Chapter 11: Preparing Your App for Release

In this chapter, we'll walk through the final steps of preparing your app for release. This includes generating signed APKs or App Bundles and creating essential assets like app icons and screenshots.

11.1 Generating Signed APKs or App Bundles: Preparing Your App for Distribution

Let's talk about how to generate signed APKs or App Bundles, which are essential steps before you can distribute your Android app to users. Signing your app ensures its authenticity and integrity.

Why Signing Your App Is Crucial

- **Authenticity:** Verifies that the app comes from you, the developer.
- **Integrity:** Ensures that the app hasn't been tampered with since it was signed.
- **Updates:** Allows users to receive updates only from the original developer.
- **Play Store Submission:** Required for publishing your app on the Google Play Store.

Understanding APKs and App Bundles

- **APK (Android Package Kit):**
  - A single file containing all the code and resources for your app.
  - Suitable for simple apps or internal distribution.

o Can result in larger download sizes for users, as it includes resources for all device configurations.

- **App Bundle (.aab):**
  o A publishing format that includes all your app's compiled code and resources.
  o Google Play's Dynamic Delivery then uses your app bundle to generate and serve optimized APKs for each user's device configuration.
  o Reduces app download sizes and optimizes delivery.
  o Required for new apps published to the Google Play Store.

Generating a Signed App Bundle (.aab)

1. **Generate a Signing Key:**
   o In Android Studio, go to Build > Generate Signed Bundle / APK.
   o Select "Android App Bundle" and click "Next."
   o Click "Create new..." to create a new keystore.
   o Fill in the keystore details (location, password, alias, etc.).
   o Remember to securely store your keystore file and passwords.
   o Click "OK."

2. **Configure Build Variants:**
   o Choose the build variant (e.g., release) for signing.
   o Enter your keystore passwords and alias.
   o Click "Next."

3. **Choose Destination Folder:**
   o Select the destination folder for the generated App Bundle.

- Choose "release" for production apps.
- Click "Finish."

4. **Locate the App Bundle:**
   - Android Studio will generate the signed App Bundle (.aab) in the specified destination folder.

Generating a Signed APK (.apk)

1. **Generate a Signing Key:**
   - Follow the same steps as above to create a keystore.

2. **Configure Build Variants:**
   - Choose the build variant (e.g., release) for signing.
   - Enter your keystore passwords and alias.
   - Click "Next."

3. **Choose Destination Folder:**
   - Select the destination folder for the generated APK.
   - Choose "release" for production apps.
   - Choose either V1 (Jar Signature), V2 (Full APK Signature), or both. V2 is recommended.
   - Click "Finish."

4. **Locate the APK:**
   - Android Studio will generate the signed APK (.apk) in the specified destination folder.

Practical Implementation: Generating a Signed App Bundle

1. **Open Android Studio:**

   o Open your Android project.

2. **Generate Signed Bundle:**

   o Go to Build > Generate Signed Bundle / APK.

   o Select "Android App Bundle" and follow the steps above.

3. **Verify the Bundle:**

   o Locate the generated .aab file in the destination folder.

   o You can use the bundletool command-line tool to analyze the App Bundle.

Generating signed App Bundles is a crucial step in the app release process. App Bundles are highly recommended for Google Play Store submissions due to their optimized delivery and reduced download sizes. Always securely store your keystore and passwords, as they are essential for updating your app. I recommend keeping multiple backups of your keystore.

Tips and Considerations:

- **Keystore Security:** Securely store your keystore and passwords.
- **Build Variants:** Use build variants to manage different build configurations (e.g., debug, release).
- **App Bundle vs. APK:** Use App Bundles for Google Play Store submissions and APKs for internal distribution or legacy devices.

- **Bundletool:** Use bundletool to analyze and test App Bundles.
- **Google Play App Signing:** Consider using Google Play App Signing for enhanced security.
- **Testing:** Thoroughly test your signed app before distributing it to users.
- **Release Notes:** Keep accurate release notes, so your users know what has changed.

Generating signed APKs or App Bundles is essential for distributing your Android app. By following the steps outlined above, you can ensure your app is authentic and ready for release. Remember to prioritize keystore security and choose the appropriate build format for your needs.

11.2 Creating App Icons and Screenshots: Visual Appeal and User Engagement

Let's talk about creating compelling app icons and screenshots. These visual elements are crucial for attracting users and conveying your app's purpose. A well-designed icon and engaging screenshots can significantly impact your app's success.

Why App Icons and Screenshots Matter

- **First Impressions:**
  - Icons are the first visual interaction users have with your app.
  - Screenshots showcase your app's features and user interface.
- **User Engagement:**

- ○ Attractive visuals can increase app downloads and user retention.
  - ○ Screenshots demonstrate the value your app provides.
- **Branding:**
  - ○ Consistent visual elements reinforce your app's brand identity.
  - ○ Helps with brand recognition.

Creating App Icons

1. **Design Principles:**
   - ○ **Simplicity:** Keep the icon clean and easily recognizable.
   - ○ **Scalability:** Design the icon in vector format (e.g., SVG) to ensure it looks sharp at all sizes.
   - ○ **Consistency:** Align the icon with your app's branding and UI design.
   - ○ **Platform Guidelines:** Follow the icon design guidelines for Android (Material Design) and other platforms.
2. **Tools:**
   - ○ **Adobe Illustrator/Photoshop:** Professional vector and raster graphics editors.
   - ○ **Figma/Sketch:** Collaborative design tools.
   - ○ **Android Studio Image Asset Studio:** Built-in tool for generating icons from vector or raster assets.
3. **Using Android Studio Image Asset Studio:**
   - ○ In Android Studio, right-click on the res folder and select New > Image Asset.
   - ○ Choose "Launcher Icons (Adaptive and Legacy)."
   - ○ Select the asset type (Image, Clip Art, Text).

- Configure the source asset and background.
- Review the generated icons and click "Finish."
- This will generate icons for different densities (mdpi, hdpi, xhdpi, etc.).

4. **Adaptive Icons:**
   - Android supports adaptive icons, which can display in various shapes on different devices.
   - Provide foreground and background layers for your icon.
   - Android Studio's Image Asset Studio makes this easy.

Creating Screenshots

1. **Showcase Key Features:**
   - Highlight the most important features and functionalities of your app.
   - Use clear and concise captions to explain each screenshot.

2. **High-Quality Images:**
   - Capture screenshots on high-resolution devices or emulators.
   - Ensure the screenshots are clear and visually appealing.

3. **Consistency:**
   - Maintain a consistent visual style across all screenshots.
   - Use consistent fonts, colors, and layouts.

4. **Tools:**
   - **Android Studio Screenshot Capture:** Built-in tool for capturing screenshots.
   - **Device Screenshots:** Capture screenshots directly on physical devices.

- ○ **Screenshot Editing Tools:** Use image editing tools to add captions and annotations.

5. **Google Play Store Requirements:**

    - ○ Follow the screenshot size and format requirements for the Google Play Store.

    - ○ Provide screenshots for different device types (phones, tablets, etc.).

Practical Implementation: Generating an Adaptive Icon

1. **Prepare an SVG:**

    - ○ Create an SVG file of your app icon using a vector graphics editor.

2. **Open Image Asset Studio:**

    - ○ In Android Studio, right-click res and select New > Image Asset.

3. **Configure Icon:**

    - ○ Select "Launcher Icons (Adaptive and Legacy)."

    - ○ Choose "Image" as the asset type and select your SVG file.

    - ○ Configure the background layer (color or image).

4. **Generate Icons:**

    - ○ Review the generated icons and click "Finish."

App icons and screenshots are your app's visual ambassadors. I've found that investing time in creating high-quality visuals pays off in increased downloads and user engagement. Adaptive icons are a must for modern Android apps. When creating screenshots, I always try to tell a story and highlight the user benefits.

Tips and Considerations:

- **A/B Testing:** Experiment with different icon designs and screenshots to see what resonates with users.

- **Localization:** Localize your screenshots and captions for different languages.

- **Update Regularly:** Update your screenshots to reflect new features and UI changes.

- **User Feedback:** Gather user feedback on your icon and screenshots.

- **Platform Specifics:** Be aware of the icon and screenshot requirements for each app store.

- **Use Mockups:** If you have a complex UI, consider using mockups to create visually appealing screenshots.

Chapter 12: Publishing Your App to the Google Play Store

You've built your app, prepared it for release, and now it's time to share it with the world. In this chapter, we'll walk through the process of publishing your app to the Google Play Store.

12.1 Creating a Google Play Developer Account: Your Gateway to the Play Store

Llet's walk through the process of creating a Google Play Developer account. This is your first step to publishing your Android apps on the Google Play Store, reaching millions of users worldwide.

Why a Google Play Developer Account?

- **App Distribution:** Enables you to publish your apps on the Google Play Store.
- **Global Reach:** Allows you to distribute your apps to a global audience.
- **Developer Tools:** Provides access to Google Play Console and other developer tools.
- **Analytics and Insights:** Offers insights into your app's performance and user engagement.

Steps to Create a Google Play Developer Account

1. **Access the Google Play Console:**
   - Open your web browser and go to play.google.com/console.
   - Sign in with your Google account. If you don't have one, create one.

2. **Agree to the Developer Distribution Agreement:**
   - Read the Google Play Developer Distribution Agreement carefully.
   - Check the box to agree to the terms.
   - Click "Continue."

3. **Pay the Registration Fee:**
   - You'll need to pay a one-time registration fee (currently $25 USD).
   - This fee allows you to publish an unlimited number of apps.
   - Provide your payment information and complete the transaction.

4. **Complete Your Account Details:**
   - Enter your developer name (this will be displayed on the Play Store).
   - Provide your contact email address.
   - Optionally, provide a website URL and phone number.
   - Fill out all the required information.

5. **Complete Developer Profile:**
   - After the payment, you will be able to fill out your developer profile. This is very important.
   - Make sure all your information is correct.

6. **Verify Your Account:**
   - Google may require you to verify your identity. Follow the instructions provided to complete the verification process.

7. **Explore the Google Play Console:**

   ○ Once your account is set up, you'll have access to the Google Play Console.

   ○ Familiarize yourself with the console's features, including:

     ■ Creating and managing apps.

     ■ Uploading APKs or App Bundles.

     ■ Managing releases.

     ■ Viewing app statistics and analytics.

     ■ Responding to user reviews.

Practical Tips and Considerations

- **Accurate Information:**

  ○ Provide accurate and up-to-date information for your developer account.

  ○ This information will be used for communication and verification purposes.

- **Secure Google Account:**

  ○ Use a strong password and enable two-factor authentication for your Google account.

  ○ This will help protect your developer account from unauthorized access.

- **Developer Name:**
  - Choose a professional and recognizable developer name.
  - This name will be visible to users on the Play Store.

- **Payment Information:**
  - Ensure your payment information is accurate and valid.
  - Keep track of your payment receipts for future reference.

- **Understanding Policies:**
  - Familiarize yourself with the Google Play Developer Program Policies.
  - Adhering to these policies is crucial for avoiding app rejections or account suspensions.

- **Account Sharing:**
  - Avoid sharing your google account with others. Google provides options within the play console to add users with specific permissions to your developer account.

Creating a Google Play Developer account is a straightforward process, but it's essential to do it correctly. The one-time fee is an investment in your app's future, allowing you to reach a massive audience. Always prioritize account security and adhere to Google's policies to ensure a smooth publishing experience. It is very important to read all of the policies before you publish your first application.

Creating a Google Play Developer account is your first step to sharing your Android apps with the world. By following these steps and tips, you'll be well on your way to publishing your apps on the Google Play Store. Remember to prioritize account security and adhere to Google's policies for a successful publishing experience.

12.2 Uploading and Publishing Your App: From Development to the Play Store

Let's guide you through the process of uploading and publishing your Android app on the Google Play Store. This is the culmination of your development efforts, making your app available to millions of users.

Why Publishing on the Play Store Matters

- **User Reach:** Distributes your app to a vast audience of Android users.
- **App Discovery:** Makes your app discoverable through search and browsing.
- **Updates and Maintenance:** Provides a platform for delivering app updates.
- **Monetization:** Enables you to monetize your app through in-app purchases or subscriptions.

Steps to Upload and Publish Your App

1. **Prepare Your App for Release:**
    - **Signed App Bundle/APK:** Ensure you have a signed App Bundle (.aab) or APK (.apk) ready for upload.
    - **App Icons and Screenshots:** Prepare high-quality app icons and screenshots according to Play Store requirements.
    - **App Metadata:** Prepare your app's title, description, and other metadata.

- ○ **Content Rating:** Determine and provide an accurate content rating for your app.
- ○ **Privacy Policy:** If your app collects user data, provide a privacy policy URL.

2. **Access the Google Play Console:**
   - ○ Log in to your Google Play Developer account at play.google.com/console.

3. **Create a New App:**
   - ○ Click the "Create app" button.
   - ○ Enter your app's name, default language, and select whether it's an app or a game.
   - ○ Choose whether it's free or paid.
   - ○ Accept the Developer Distribution Agreement and click "Create app."

4. **Upload Your App Bundle/APK:**
   - ○ Go to the "Releases" section in the left navigation menu.
   - ○ Select the release track (e.g., Internal testing, Closed testing, Open testing, Production).
   - ○ Click "Create new release."
   - ○ Upload your signed App Bundle (.aab) or APK (.apk).
   - ○ Add release notes describing the changes in this version.

5. **Complete Store Listing:**
   - ○ Go to the "Store presence" section and select "Main store listing."
   - ○ Enter your app's short description, full description, and add screenshots.
   - ○ Add your app's icon, feature graphic, and video (if applicable).
   - ○ Choose your app's category and tags.
   - ○ Provide your contact details (email, website, phone number).

6. **Set Content Rating:**
   - Go to the "Store presence" section and select "Content rating."
   - Complete the content rating questionnaire accurately.
   - Calculate and apply the content rating.

7. **Set Pricing and Distribution:**
   - Go to the "Monetize" section and select "Pricing & distribution."
   - Choose whether your app is free or paid.
   - Select the countries where you want to distribute your app.
   - Configure any other distribution settings (e.g., device exclusions).

8. **Review and Rollout Release:**
   - Go back to the "Releases" section and select your release track.
   - Review your release details and click "Review release."
   - If everything looks good, click "Start rollout to production" (or "Rollout" for other tracks).

9. **Monitor Your App:**
   - After publishing, monitor your app's performance in the Google Play Console.
   - Respond to user reviews and ratings.
   - Track your app's download and usage statistics.
   - Provide updates as needed.

Practical Tips and Considerations

- **Thorough Testing:**
  - Test your app thoroughly on various devices and Android versions before publishing.

- **Accurate Metadata:**
  - Provide accurate and compelling app descriptions and metadata.
- **High-Quality Visuals:**
  - Use high-resolution app icons and screenshots.
- **Release Notes:**
  - Always provide detailed release notes for each update.
- **Content Rating Accuracy:**
  - Provide an accurate content rating to avoid app rejections.
- **User Feedback:**
  - Pay attention to user feedback and reviews.
- **Staged Rollouts:**
  - Use staged rollouts to gradually release updates to users.
- **Policy Compliance:**
  - Ensure your app complies with Google Play Developer Program Policies.
- **A/B Testing:**
  - Google Play allows A/B testing of your store listing. Take advantage of this.

Publishing your app is an exciting milestone. I've found that paying close attention to metadata, visuals, and user feedback is crucial for app success. Remember to use staged rollouts for production releases, so you can monitor for any unexpected issues. It is also very important to respond to user reviews, to show that you care about your users.

Uploading and publishing your app on the Google Play Store is a multi-step process that requires careful attention to detail. By following these steps and tips, you can successfully publish your app and reach a global audience. Remember to prioritize user experience and continuously monitor your app's performance.

Conclusion: Mastering Android Development in the Modern Era

We've journeyed through the intricate landscape of Android development, from setting up your environment to publishing your app on the Google Play Store. Along the way, we've explored the power of Jetpack Compose, the importance of robust state management, the intricacies of network requests, and the critical role of thorough testing.

Key Takeaways and Insights

- **Jetpack Compose: A Paradigm Shift:**
  - Jetpack Compose has revolutionized Android UI development. Its declarative approach empowers developers to create beautiful and responsive UIs with less code.
  - Embracing Compose means embracing a more intuitive and efficient way to build Android apps.
- **State Management: The Heart of Your App:**
  - Effective state management using ViewModel and StateFlow is paramount for building robust and maintainable apps.
  - Understanding how to manage UI state ensures your app remains consistent and responsive to user interactions.
- **Network Requests: Connecting to the World:**
  - Integrating with APIs and fetching data from the web is essential for creating dynamic and engaging apps.
  - Retrofit and Kotlin Coroutines provide powerful tools for making network requests efficiently.

- **Testing: Ensuring Quality and Reliability:**
  - Thorough testing on both emulators and physical devices is crucial for delivering a high-quality app.
  - Debugging tools in Android Studio are invaluable for identifying and fixing issues.[6]

- **Publishing: Reaching a Global Audience:**
  - Generating signed App Bundles and publishing on the Google Play Store allows you to share your app with millions of users.
  - Following best practices for app icons, screenshots, and metadata is essential for app discoverability and user engagement.

- **The Importance of Continuous Learning:**
  - Android development is a dynamic field, and staying up-to-date with the latest technologies and best practices is crucial.
  - Embrace continuous learning and experimentation to improve your skills and build better apps.

Throughout this journey, I've emphasized the importance of understanding core concepts, writing clean and maintainable code, and prioritizing user experience. Android development is not just about writing code; it's about creating meaningful experiences for users.

I've also highlighted the significance of using the right tools and techniques for each task. Jetpack Compose, for example, has significantly simplified UI

development, while ViewModel and StateFlow have made state management more manageable.

Remember that every app is unique, and there's always room for innovation and creativity. Don't be afraid to experiment, explore new technologies, and push the boundaries of what's possible.

Looking Ahead

As Android continues to evolve, new technologies and best practices will emerge. Embrace these changes, stay curious, and continue to learn. Your dedication to crafting high-quality Android apps will be appreciated by the users that use them.

Thank you for joining me on this exploration of Android development. I hope this guide has provided you with valuable insights and practical knowledge.